AYCKBOURN

S0-BQS-003

in an hour

E. TERESA CHOATE

SUSAN C. MOORE, SERIES EDITOR

PLAYWRIGHTS in an hour

know the playwright, love the play

IN AN HOUR BOOKS • HANOVER, NEW HAMPSHIRE • INANHOURBOOKS.COM
AN IMPRINT OF SMITH AND KRAUS PUBLISHERS, INC • SMITHANDKRAUS.COM

With grateful thanks to Carl R. Mueller,
whose fascinating introductions to his translations of the Greek and
German playwrights provided inspiration for this series.

Published by In an Hour Books
an imprint of Smith and Kraus, Inc.
177 Lyme Road, Hanover, NH 03755
inanhourbooks.com SmithandKraus.com

Know the playwright, love the play.

In an Hour, In a Minute, and Theater IQ are registered trademarks of
In an Hour Books.

ABSURD PERSON SINGULAR. © 1974 by Haydonning Ltd. Reprinted by permission of Casarotto
    Ramsay Assoc. Ltd. For performance rights, contact Samuel French, Inc.
    (www.samuelfrench.com) (212-206-8990).
INTIMATE EXCHANGES. © 1985 by Haydonning Ltd. Reprinted by permission of Casarotto Ramsay
    Assoc. Ltd. For performance rights, contact Samuel French, Inc. (www.samuelfrench.com)
    (212-206-8990).
LIVING TOGETHER (THE NORMAN CONQUESTS). © 1975 by Haydonning Ltd. Reprinted by permis-
    sion of Casarotto Ramsay Assoc. Ltd. For performance rights, contact Samuel French, Inc.
    (www.samuelfrench.com) (212-206-8990).
PRIVATE FEARS IN PUBLIC PLACES. © 2006 by Haydonning Ltd. Reprinted by permission of Faber
    and Faber/Farrar, Straus & Giroux. For performance rights, contact Samuel French, Inc.
    (www.samuelfrench.com) (212-206-8990).

Front cover design by Dan Mehling, dmehling@gmail.com
Text design by Kate Mueller, Electric Dragon Productions
Book production by Dede Cummings Design, DCDesign@sover.net

ISBN-13: 978-1-936232-02-4
ISBN-10: 1-936232-02-2
Library of Congress Control Number: 2009943226

CONTENTS

Why Playwrights in an Hour?

This new series by Smith and Kraus Publishers titled Playwrights in an Hour has a dual purpose for being; one academic, the other general. For the general reader, this volume, as well as the many others in the series, offers in compact form the information needed for a basic understanding and appreciation of the works of each volume's featured playwright. Which is not to say that there don't exist volumes on end devoted to each playwright under consideration. But inasmuch as few are blessed with enough time to read the splendid scholarship that is available, a brief, highly focused accounting of the playwright's life and work is in order.

The central feature of the series, a thirty- to forty-page essay, integrates the playwright into the context of his or her time and place. And the volumes, though written to high standards of academic integrity, are accessible in style and approach to the general reader as well as to the student, and of course to the theater professional and theatergoer.

These books will serve for the brushing up of one's knowledge of a playwright's career, to the benefit of theater work or theatergoing. The Playwrights in an Hour series represents all periods of Western theater: Aeschylus to Shakespeare to Wedekind to Ibsen to Williams to Beckett, and on to the great contemporary playwrights who continue to offer joy and enlightenment to a grateful world.

Carl R. Mueller
School of Theater, Film and Television
Department of Theater
University of California, Los Angeles

Introduction

Alan Ayckbourn may be the most well rounded man of the theater since Molière. Best known as a playwright, he has also functioned as a director, actor, stage manager, and sound designer. And let us not forget his tenure as artistic director of a major theater in Scarborough. He has also written over a hundred plays for different venues — stage, radio, and children's theater — making him among the most prolific dramatists since Spain's sixteenth-century Lope De Vega (who wrote over 1800 plays).

Ayckbourn continues in the tradition of British farceurs that has included Benn Levey, Ben Travers, and Frederick Lonsdale. That tradition later found its way into radio and TV in *The Goon Show* (broadcast 1951–60) and *Monte Python's Flying Circus* (broadcast 1969–74).

Conscious of the tradition he was working in, Ayckbourn cites Oscar Wilde and Noel Coward among his influences. Also, if his adaptation of Richard Brinsley Sheridan's *A Trip to Scarborough* (1777) is any indication, he even sees the great Irish farce masters of the eighteenth century, from the precocious Richard Brinsley Richardson to the simple-hearted Oliver Goldsmith, as inspirations.

Where his work departs from theirs, and seems more akin to such contemporary farces as Michael Frayn's *Noises Off* (1982), is in the almost geometric nature of the plotting. His plays are nothing if not well-made. They would have impressed an architectural engineer. He has written plays with sixteen possible endings (*Intimate Exchanges,* 1982) and in three different time periods (*A Trip to Scarborough,* 1982). For instance, in *How the Other Half Loves* (1969), he throws two different dinner parties on stage simultaneously, though they take place on two different evenings. In *The Norman Conquests* (1973), he gives us three plays revolving around the same action, each occurring simultaneously in three different locations. And in *Bedroom Farce* (1975), he brings on stage three separate bedrooms, all at the same time, where three (later four) actions are being performed before the audience simultaneously.

Perhaps the most intricate of these mechanisms is his more recent *House &Garden* (1999). Each play — *House* and *Garden* — has one cast and is performed simultaneously on adjacent stages. This results in a merry race as actors, running from stage to stage, have as much trouble retracing their routes as remembering their lines. Their greater purpose is to make certain that both plays take exactly two-and-one-half hours to perform. One can almost hear the metronome ticking.

As sometimes happens in Ayckbourn's more mechanical inventions, the gimmick does the work of the imagination. As for the content, Kenneth Tynan, the acerbic theater critic for *The Observer,* and later Sir Laurence Olivier's Literary Manager, once wrote a piece called "The Lost Art of Bad Drama," in which, no doubt thinking partly of Ayckbourn, he imagined a generic "Loamshire Play." He writes, "at no point may the plot or characters make more than a superficial contact with reality. Characters earning less than 1000 pounds a year should be restricted to small parts. . . . Women should declare themselves by running the palm of one hand up their victims lapel and saying . . . 'Let's face it, Arthur, you're not exactly indifferent to me.'"

While the plays of Alan Ayckbourn do depend heavily on the conventions of middle class suburbia, they depend even more on Alan Ayckbourn's wit, humanity, and unfailing good nature. And also on his capacity to occasionally have something serious in his sights, such as the failings of Prime Minister Thatcher's administration. Ultimately, the greatness of Ayckbourn's plays lie in the genius of his farcical and mischievous mind.

Robert Brustein
Founding Director of the Yale and American Repertory Theatres
Distinguishing Scholar in Residence, Suffolk University
Senior Research Fellow, Harvard University

Ayckbourn

IN A MINUTE

A snapshot of the playwright's world. From historical events to pop-culture and the literary landscape of the time, this brief list catalogues events that directly or indirectly impacted the playwright's writing. Play citations refer to openings or premieres.

Ayckbourn

HIS WORKS

DRAMATIC WORKS

The Square Cat

Love After All

Standing Room Only

Countdown, one-act

Mr. Whatnot

Meet My Father, retitled *Relatively Speaking*

The Sparrow

How the Other Half Loves

The Story So Far, retitled *Me Times Me Times Me*, retitled *Family Circles*

Time and Time Again

Absurd Person Singular

The Norman Conquests: Living Together (formerly *Make Yourself at Home*), *Table Manners* (originally *Fancy Meeting You*), *Round and Round the Garden*

Absent Friends

Confusions: "Mother Figure," "Drinking Companion," "Between Mouthfuls," "Gosforth's Fete," "A Talk in the Park"

Jeeves, musical (with Andrew Lloyd Webber)

Bedroom Farce

Just Between Ourselves

Ten Times Table

Joking Apart

Sisterly Feelings

Taking Steps

Suburban Strains, musical (with Paul Todd)

Season's Greetings

This section presents a complete list of the playwright's works in chronological order by world premiere date.

FAMILY AND CHILDREN'S PLAYS

Dad's Tale

Christmas V Mastermind

Ernie's Incredible Illucinations

Mr. A's Amazing Maze Plays

The Inside Outside Slide Show

Invisible Friends

This Is Where We Came In

Callisto 5

My Very Own Story

The Musical Jigsaw Play, a play with music (with John Pattison)

The Champion of Paribanou

The Boy Who Fell into a Book

Gizmo

Callisto #7

Whenever, musical (with Denis King)

The Jollies

The Princess and the Mouse

The Ten Magic Bridges

Orvin — Champion of Champions, musical (with Denis King)

My Sister Sadie

Miranda's Magic Mirror

Miss Yesterday

The Girl Who Lost Her Voice

Awaking Beauty

Winnie's Wonderful Day

REVUES/MUSICAL ENTERTAINMENTS

Men on Women on Men (with Paul Todd)

First Course (with Paul Todd)

Second Helping (with Paul Todd)

Me, Myself & I (with Paul Todd)

Incidental Music (with Paul Todd)

The 7 Deadly Virtues (with Paul Todd)

The Westwoods (with Paul Todd)
Boy Meets Girl (with Paul Todd)
Girl Meets Boy (with Paul Todd)
Mere Soup Songs (with Paul Todd)
Cheap and Cheerful (with Denis King)

TELEVISION PLAYS
Service Not Included
A Cut in Rates

BOOK
The Crafty Art of Playmaking

POETRY
In *Occasional Poets: An Anthology*. Edited by Richard Adams. London:
Viking, 1986.

Onstage with Ayckbourn

*Introducing Colleagues and
Contemporaries of Alan Ayckbourn*

 THEATER

Peter Brook, English director
Peter Hall, English director
Arthur Miller, American playwright
Joe Orton, English playwright
Harold Pinter, English playwright
Neil Simon, American playwright
Tom Stoppard, British playwright
August Wilson, American playwright

 ARTS

The Beatles, English musicians
Bob Dylan, American musician
David Hockney, English painter
Zubin Mehta, Indian conductor
Rudolf Nureyev, Russian dancer
Luciano Pavarotti, Italian singer
Elvis Presley, American singer
Andy Warhol, American pop artist

 FILM

Woody Allen, American filmmaker
Sean Connery, Scottish actor
Bernardo Bertolucci, Italian filmmaker
Werner Herzog, German filmmaker

This section lists contemporaries whom the playwright may or may not have known.

Marilyn Monroe, American film star
Martin Scorsese, American filmmaker
Peter Sellers, English comedian and actor
François Truffaut, French filmmaker

POLITICS/MILITARY

Tony Blair, British prime minister
Bill Clinton, American president
Elizabeth II, queen of England
Mikhail Gorbachev, U.S.S.R. political leader
Saddam Hussein, Iraqi president
Georges Pompidou, French president
Margaret Thatcher, British prime minister
Desmond Tutu, South African bishop and political activist

SCIENCE

Joan Goodall, English zoologist
Stephen Jay Gould, American paleontologist
Stephen Hawking, English astrophysicist
R. D. Laing, Scottish psychiatrist
Richard Leakey, Kenyan archaeologist
Marshall Nirenberg, American geneticist
Carl Sagan, American astronomer
James Watson, American biochemist

LITERATURE

Maya Angelou, American poet
Truman Capote, American writer
Joan Didion, American writer
Vaclav Havel, Czech writer and president
Seamus Heaney, Irish poet
Allen Ginsberg, American poet
Gabriel García Márquez, Colombian writer
Elie Wiesel, Romanian/American writer

RELIGION/PHILOSOPHY

Isaiah Berlin, Latvian/British philosopher
Albert Camus, Algerian/French philosopher
Jacques Derrida, Algerian/French philosopher
Michel Foucault, French philosopher and historian
14th Dalai Lama, Tibetan religious leader
Billy Graham, American evangelist
Ayatollah Ruhollah Khomeini, Iranian iman
Pope John Paul II, Polish pope

SPORTS

Muhammad Ali, American boxer
David Beckham, English soccer player
Wilt Chamberlain, American basketball player
Sir Nick Faldo, British golfer
Kareem Abdul Jabbar, American basketball player
Willie Mays, American baseball player
Martina Navratilova, Czech/American tennis player
Pelé, Brazilian soccer player

INDUSTRY/BUSINESS

Warren Buffet, American investor
William (Bill) Gates III, American business magnate
Carlos Slim Helú, Mexican telecommunications businessman
Lee Iacocca, American businessman
Rubert Murdoch, Australian media mogul
Amancio Ortego, Spanish entrepreneur
Ted Turner, American entrepreneur, media mogul
Donald Trump, American real estate developer

AYCKBOURN

in an hour

WHERE'S THE RESPECT?

Alan Ayckbourn, best known for his frolicsome farces and comedies, does not always receive the respect afforded such contemporaries as Harold Pinter and Tom Stoppard. Ayckbourn himself observed in *The Crafty Art of Playmaking*: "I have a theory that to be genuinely respectable as a so-called comic writer, on par with an equivalent 'serious' writer, you need to have been dead preferably for a century. By which time, of course, most of the comedy is incomprehensible and can only be laughed at by scholars. Never mind, rejoice in the fact that should you be fortunate enough to write comedy, you'll do very nicely during your own lifetime if you're lucky, and to hell with posterity. Though ironically, if you write comedy truthfully and honestly, it is possible that the play might still survive because of its truth of observation, long after most of the surface jokes are dead."

He writes about the personal, even when addressing the political, and is not given to intellectualizing or research. As he further

This is the core of the book. The essay places the playwright in the context of his or her world and analyzes the influences and inspirations within that world.

observed: "Often we quite wrongly suspect simplicity. We go digging around in the creative sand trying to make our art more meaningful, somehow 'deeper'. Generally all we do is end up with our heads entirely buried, presenting the audience with our rear ends."

His plays do not read as well as they play — they must be seen to be fully appreciated. Although often compared to Neil Simon, aside from the fact that they are both wildly successful comic playwrights, their comedy differs. Ayckbourn said it best in Albert E. Kalson's *Laughter in the Dark:* "If you dropped a play of his in the street and the pages fell out in any old order, you'd still be laughing as you picked them up. If you dropped a play of mine, too bad. As a writer, he's highly verbal whereas I'm situational."

In addition, audience members and critics often have preconceived notions about what he *should* be writing. Everyone seems to long for what his biographer, Paul Allen, calls the "Ayckbourn roar," that moment when the audience is laughing so loudly that the actors must simply stop talking and wait it out in character.

He has been called the bard of the English bourgeoisie, the Molière and Nöel Coward of the middle class. Like Molière, his essence is humor and social commentary; like Coward he writes wittily and very quickly. He has also been compared to Anton Chekhov. Like Chekhov, his characters are going about their day-to-day activities while their lives are shown to be void of any real meaning, and the central action is often kept offstage, as onstage we see the results of or reactions to the offstage action.

In his insightful analysis of Ayckbourn's works, Kalson succinctly summarizes central questions found in the canon: "Do husbands have the ethical license to dictate the behavior of their wives? Do corporate executives have the right to manipulate the lives of their underlings? Do world leaders have the power of life and death over their subjects? . . . Are there no bounds to man's grabs for control of his universe? Can man ultimately play God?"

ONE-MAN RENAISSANCE

He has written over one hundred scripts of various types: adult plays, family plays, children's plays, adaptations, musicals, and revues. His plays are often difficult to classify. While farce plays an important part in his earlier plays, his characters are usually more developed — so where does farce end and comedy begin? Furthermore, as he matured, his plays grew darker, and comedy bedded with tragedy. The pantheon of his characters includes those who demolish the status quo and cause chaos, oblivious men and unsatisfied women, mild and manic characters set in contrast. His plot devices include space and time manipulation, multiple choice, and alternate realities.

While his characters are undeniably British, his scripts have been performed worldwide and translated into over thirty languages. He is credited with helping resuscitate commercial theater in England and has been awarded numerous recognitions and honors.

Despite being a wildly successful playwright, he has spent much of his time directing, usually premiering his own plays and directing those of others. From 1972 to 2009, he was also a highly successful and respected artistic director, running his own theater on the coast of England. He expanded the theater from a summer tourist attraction to a yearround, integral part of the community. For many years the next London hit was likely to be one of his plays that premiered the year before in Scarborough. His biographer calculated that since 1970, Ayckbourn has spent a mere 10 percent of any given year writing plays.

LOVE CHILD

His mother's father, Joseph William Worley, was a Shakespearean actor; her mother, Lillian, had been a male impersonator in English music halls before entering the legitimate theater. The man who would become Ayckbourn's father, Horace Ayckbourn, was a violinist and a regular visitor to Worley's home, where his mother, Irene Maud Worley, was a thirteen-year-old aspiring writer.

Her first lover was Michael Joseph, a literary agent who was instrumental in launching her career. Her first husband was Neville Monroe, a young man with a monocle who said he was in the film business. They married in 1930, when she was twenty-four. She ended up supporting him and shortly sent him packing.

She then became involved with Horace Ayckbourn, now the first violinist of the London Symphony Orchestra. She claimed that they had married, but this was untrue. (Ayckbourn himself did not learn of this until 1991, when his stepfather, Cecil Pye, revealed that to marry him she had had to divorce her first husband, Neville.) She became pregnant in 1938 and, although she wanted an abortion, Horace dissuaded her. They lived in London, she writing in the kitchen, he practicing in the sitting room. On April 12, 1939, as Horace was playing in the pit orchestra at the Lyceum, she gave birth to Alan. Adhering to the principle that the "show must go on," Horace was not informed of his son's birth until after the performance. Ayckbourn has no memory of the three of them living together as a family in London. Their relationship seems to have broken up in stages as Horace repeatedly went after other women. Eventually he ran off for good with the second violinist.

A SOUTHERNER

Soon after the end of the war, he and his mother moved to a garden-surrounded cottage in Sussex, to the south of London. Here she supported them by writing, mostly romantic short stories for magazines. She typed on her Underwood typewriter while little Alan pounded away on a little typewriter she gave him when he was six.

At seven he attended his first school at a convent across the street from where he and his mother lived. Between the nuns and around 150 girls in the school, Alan and the few boys that attended were considerably outnumbered. He did not want to stay. When he defaced his books after being forbidden to listen to *Dick Barton: Special Agent* on the radio, his mother pulled him out and sent him to an all-boys boarding school, Wisborough Lodge. The seven-year-old Alan lived there even though it was a short walk to his home.

The post-war British boarding school featured wretched food, unheated dormitories, outdoor bathrooms, compulsory sports year-round, and male teachers who ran the gamut from drunk sadists to saints of education. Desperately unhappy at first and missing his mother, young Alan wet his bed and was often ill. However, it was considered proper to suppress one's emotions. Eventually he adjusted.

He appeared in his first school play at Wisborough. Like his mother, he was submitting works for publication, selling a poem, "The Moon," to a children's magazine. He wrote his first play (based on the popular comic novels of Anthony Buckeridge) about two middle-class English schoolboys, their friends, and assorted schoolmasters.

Occasionally his father showed up in an open roadster wearing a pilot-style cap. During school holidays when he was older, he visited his father, who had taken early retirement and moved with his new wife (the second violinist) to a cottage in rural Norwich. Father and son discovered that they both had the same sense of humor. They also shared a love of board games. In fact, Ayckbourn's love of the intricacies of games would later manifest itself in his more complex play structures.

One day when he was at school, he received a letter from his mother announcing that she was getting remarried. In 1948, she married Cecil Pye, a bank manager. Alan did not attend. He met his stepfather after the honeymoon, politely shaking his hand. He also acquired a younger stepbrother, Christopher. They lived in a series of apartments above banks in Sussex. The newlyweds' personalities were vastly divergent, and the marriage was quite contentious, both verbally and physically.

SPORTS, GOD, COLD BATHS, AND THEATER

In 1952, at thirteen years old, he received a Barclay's Bank scholarship to Haileybury and Imperial Service College in Herefordshire (the equivalent of a middle and high school in the United States). This public school differed greatly from his previous private boarding school. Haileybury was in the British tradition of stringent authority, with lots of turning-boys-into-men exercises: cold morning baths, strict rules and regulations, sports, military exercises, and a well-laid-out Sunday tea. Corporal punishment was also part of this training, and he received a few beatings from the housemaster. Confirmation classes in the Church of England begin around the same time as puberty. Being encouraged to think about God and sin, combined with cold baths, was thought to be an excellent means of subduing adolescent urges.

In addition to regular academic fare, there was film viewing (he liked Nöel Coward's *Blithe Spirit*) and theatricals, such as the comic revues performed by his "house" at the end of each school term, some written by Ayckbourn. He also wrote plays emulating Pirandello and Ionesco. He tried his hand at what became known as the "angry young man" plays, which he called the "damn you, mother" genre. As the editor of his house magazine, he learned to write quickly. Having trouble commissioning articles, he wrote many of them himself, typing through the night.

His French teacher, Edgar Matthews, adored theater and focused his considerable energies on directing plays. In 1954, when Alan was fifteen, he was cast as Peter in *Romeo and Juliet.* They toured the production to Holland, where the boys indulged in a lot of underage drinking. In 1955, at sixteen, he was cast as Macduff in *Macbeth* and toured the United States and Canada. For this production, girls were brought in to play the female roles.

Upon returning to complete his final year, Ayckbourn turned to Matthews for help; he wanted to be an actor. Matthews used his one major professional theater contact to get the seventeen-year-old Ayckbourn a job as an assistant stage manager and a walk-on with Sir Donald Wolfit's company at the 1956 Edinburgh Festival. Ayckbourn leapt at the chance, leaving behind an extension of his scholarship and a university education.

Before departing for Scotland, Ayckbourn took part in the end-of-term variety show and performed in a farce. In this production he experienced the exhilaration of sending an audience into gales of laughter, with a standing ovation and cheering at the end. While acting was not to be his ultimate destiny, it is significant that audience-pleasing, often comic, playwriting was.

MEETING GIRLS

Ayckbourn has said that he got involved in theater to meet girls. Obviously the experience of touring North America with actresses had made an impression, although his love of performance and writing was already well established.

At the Edinburgh Festival with Wolfit, Ayckbourn, in addition to being the go-to guy and prop master, also played a Spanish soldier. At the costume inspection, Wolfit thought that the military hat made Ayckbourn look funny. But rather than cut the actor, Wolfit threw history out the window and cut all the hats, much to the costume designer's dismay. Wolfit, one of the last of the actor-managers, taught Ayckbourn a lesson he never forgot the performance was all — no audience, no theater.

Back in London after his three weeks in Scotland, he found another internship with the Connaught Theatre in Worthing. He was again an assistant stage manager/actor. He made props, painted the sets, served tea, and fed the theater's cat. He played small parts and once got to go on for a juvenile lead who had skipped town.

He spent the second half of the season with Hazel Vincent Wallace's Repertory Company in Leatherhead. Liking his looks, Wallace gave him better roles than he had experienced at Connaught, such as Jimmy Curry in N. Richard Nash's *The Rainmaker*. He learned some valuable basics of acting, including stage makeup and staying physically open to the audience. As an assistant stage manager, he became involved with developing sound effects, which became a lifelong interest.

ROUND AND ROUND

In several of Acykbourn's plays (*Intimate Exchanges*, for instance), it is a little decision that results in the course of one's life. Such was the case when the season ended and he was asked if he wanted to work as the stage manager at Stephen Joseph's theater-in-the-round for the summer season in the Scarborough seaside resort. Ayckbourn didn't know what theater-in-the-round was. Few did. Stephen Joseph, having seen circle staging in American universities, is credited with introducing it to England. He was, in fact, quite messianic about it.

Ayckbourn went to see a production of Jean-Paul Sartre's *No Exit* that was being performed by the company in London. The close proximity of the audience to the actors brought the sexual tension inherent in Sartre's play viscerally home to the young man. So he boarded a train to Scarborough. In the London *Times* (July 21, 2008), Ayckbourn recalled, "I remember I got off the train packed with holidaymakers and this bracing air and smell of chips. I said, 'Wow!' Because I was an inland child living in north Sussex, one of the great treats as a child was a trip to the seaside — so, dear reader, I bought the sweet shop. I came to the seaside and stayed." And on top of being a full-fledged stage manager, he was to play a good role in J. B. Priestly's *An Inspector Calls*, that of Eric Birling, the "not quite at ease, half-shy, half-assertive" son of the family. It was a company where everyone did everything. Hours were long and he loved it.

As Ayckbourn would write almost exclusively for this theater, it is important to understand theater-in-the-round. A centrally located stage with the audience sitting around it on four sides has limited space for scenery, as audience sightlines would be blocked. The characters are allowed much more natural movement and placement, as opposed to proscenium staging, where the actors must turn out to the audience. Joseph maintained that by removing the artificial barrier of the proscenium arch, the actor was fully exposed and had to be far more truthful. In this medium, the playwright and the director were very much in the service of the actors and the audience. In Ian Watson's *Conversations with Ayckbourn*, Ayckbourn, echoing Joseph, observed, "the only thing that mattered about theatre, when it came to it, was the actor and the audience. This was the most important concept and the round, more than any other medium, emphasizes this most strongly. The actor is in the middle and the audience surrounds him and there's nothing else, really."

Located in a converted concert room in the town library, the theater had an acting area of fourteen feet by eighteen feet. There were only two entrances for actors to enter the playing space, so until the company moved into their new space in 1976, the dozens of plays Ayckbourn would later write for the library space had to accommodate only two entrances.

When his plays transferred to proscenium stages in London, it sometimes resulted in less successful productions. *Ten Times Table*, in which a bunch of contentious committee members effectively faced each other across a table in Scarborough, was not so effective on the West End proscenium stage, where they had to angle out toward the audience.

MENTOR AND SPIRITUAL HOME

The decision to take the job in Scarborough brought Ayckbourn into the orbit of the man who was most instrumental in his future career, Stephen Joseph. Ironically, Joseph was the son of Michael Joseph, the man with whom Ayckbourn's mother had had a long affair.

Their first meeting was reminiscent of farcical scenes Ayckbourn would so brilliantly write later. The old lighting systems were monstrous and had large levers. Achieving a full stage blackout seemed to require more hands and feet than the typical stage manager possessed. Ayckbourn was struggling with the board when he became aware of a tall man standing behind him, who proceeded to demonstrate a better way to do it. Helpfully, he grabbed a length of wood, laid it across the levers and lowered all the dimmers at once, resulting in a full stage blackout. Of course, the actors were still mid-scene and required light, not darkness. Ayckbourn later described Joseph as both genius and madman. But it was the inspired madness of a true devotee, one who felt passionately about theater-in-the-round and new scripts. Joseph also believed that one should be *un homme de théâtre*. So Ayckbourn not only acted and stage-managed, but was also involved in all aspects of production except costume construction, most especially lighting and sound design.

PLAYWRIGHT, HUSBAND, FATHER, DIRECTOR

In 1958, he complained to Stephen Joseph about the parts he was getting. Joseph responded that Ayckbourn should write a play with a role for himself. The result was *The Square Cat*, which he wrote with a fetching actress in the company, Christine Roland. They wrote it in two weeks, a pattern of quick writing that Ayckbourn would continue to practice. It was produced in the 1959 summer season with Ayckbourn in the starring role.

It is the story of a hot and sexy rock 'n' roll star named Jerry Wattis (Alan could neither play the guitar nor sing). An older woman in an unhappy marriage arranges to meet with him in secret. Her enraged husband shows up, as does her not-very-bright son, and her lovely daughter. It turns out that the rock-and-roll rage is actually a sweet young man named Arthur Brummage, who promptly falls in love with the daughter. Approximately 2,000 audience members saw it; reviewers liked his performance, but no one announced the arrival of the next Nöel Coward. However, his career as a professional playwright was underway.

After Ayckbourn wrote two other plays produced by the company, Joseph requested a play about overpopulation. The result was the 1961 *Standing Room Only*, not so much about overpopulation as about intrusive government control. It concerns a gridlock that is so terminal that people are now living in their vehicles. The setting is a double-decker bus where the driver and his family reside with passengers as "houseguests." One daughter breaks the law and gets pregnant. A producer wanted to take *Standing Room Only* to London. Ayckbourn rewrote it several times in an attempt to make it meet West End demands for plays with one or two star parts. It never fit the bill. But the play did get him a literary agent, one of the most influential in England, Margaret (Peggy) Ramsay.

These first plays had been written under the pseudonym of Roland Allen, a combination of his and Christine Roland's name. During the 1958 summer season, he had become engaged to two women. In *The Independent* (August 24, 2008), Ayckbourn explained, "Coming from public school, you never even saw a girl. I was so desperate to get married I proposed to anybody. I broke off one engagement, and found myself in the pub the next night proposing to someone else. The ring wasn't even cold from the other finger." Christine Roland was the "someone else." After the fall tour, they spent a joyous, white Christmas together. The engagement stuck, especially when Christine became pregnant. They married the following year, in 1959, and their first son, Steven, was born in December, named after Stephen Joseph. He and Christine were poor; only the support of her parents and occasional financial help from his mother made it possible for Ayckbourn to remain working for Joseph. By the end of 1960, there was another child on the way. In the summer of 1961, his second son, Philip, was born.

To acting, stage-managing, writing, marriage, and fatherhood, Ayckbourn now added directing. In 1961, Joseph asked Ayckbourn to direct Patrick Hamilton's *Gaslight*, a suspense melodrama about a husband trying to convince his wife that she is going mad. The play is a combination of humor and suspense, two elements that Ayckbourn soon perfected in his own plays.

He was twenty-two years old.

INFLUENCES

By this stage in his life, the groundwork had been laid for the remarkable canon of plays to come.

As noted, his plays are populated by a plethora of unhappy women and obtuse men: comic characters who become tragic figures. The shadow of his mother can be seen in the cave of his creative mind. Versions of Ayckbourn himself show up more frequently. His mother was a deeply flawed but determined woman supporting herself and her son through writing. Ayckbourn is known for his sympathetic portrayal of women. And there was the occasional father, showing up handsome and romantic in his roadster. Many of the men in his plays would be equally endearing but ultimately infuriating. Both his mother's and father's affairs found their way into the many unfaithful characters he created (and into his own behavior). His mother's second marriage and his own troubled marriage are reflected in his scripts' many conflicted couples. As Ayckbourn revealed in *The New York Times* (March 25, 1979): "I was surrounded by relationships that weren't altogether stable, the air was often blue, and things were sometimes flying across the kitchen."

Ayckbourn's time at school also had its impact. The all-important suppression of emotions so valued at English boarding schools and by English society as a whole was to play an important part in the workings of Ayckbourn's plays, where the polite and oh-so-correct restrained response to even the most outrageous circumstances often provided the foundation for his comedy.

Elements of radio shows he loved growing up also influenced his writing. *The Goon Show* was a particular favorite, featuring wildly comic parodies of popular adventure stories. A typical line from the *Scarlet Capsule* episode suggests the appeal it held for a young man: "Seagoon: We can't stand around here doing nothing. People will think we're workmen!" He also adored film, and seems to have been particularly influenced by Saturday morning children's serials, the silent films of Buster Keaton and Harold Lloyd, the films of D. W. Griffith, and thriller/mysteries.

His plays also reflect two regional influences: his southern Sussex upbringing and his many years in Scarborough on the northeast coast. His plays often capture the middle-class people of the south, their speech patterns and their style. He sets several of his plays in Pendon, his fictitious village set in southern England, which becomes home for flawed people in a flawed world. As Ayckbourn observed in a January 5, 1976, London *Times* article: "I spent all my childhood up to the age of about seventeen in the Home Countries, Sussex mainly, and I think that's where you get your stamp from, that's the filter. I suppose I suck in things, but it always gets filtered through my southern interpreter, somewhere in my head." After moving to Scarborough, he encountered the north, an area known for its bluntness. In an interview in the London *Times* (May 5, 1976), Ayckbourn described the seaside resort: "The easiest way to get about is walking or busing. . . . which means that I spend all my time overhearing by accident." And it is this happy eavesdropping that provides more material for his plays.

Of course, Ayckbourn was an actor before he dedicated himself to writing and directing. His biographer, Paul Allen, notes that the "gang of four" (Pinter, Osborne, Wesker, and Ayckbourn) had all acted before they became playwrights and understood the practical necessity of keeping the audience engaged during a performance. Having played around fifty roles in circle staging by the time he retired from acting at the age of twenty-five, Ayckbourn also understood the particular demands of in-the-round staging. One acting experience had a particular impact on his writing. During the 1959–60 winter season, Joseph brought in Harold Pinter to direct his play *The Birthday Party*. Pinter cast Ayckbourn as Stanley, the birthday boy who is overcome and taken away by the two gangsters. Ayckbourn considers this experience a turning point in his career. As he noted in *The New York Times* (January 28, 1990): "It was the first time I had seen seriousness and humor juxtaposed quite so closely." He also acknowledged another connection to Pinter in the London *Times* (January 5, 1976): "He writes rather like poets in that his use of words is very specific. He has a love of distorting the everyday phrase, slightly bending it. He bends it more than I do, but I also bend phrases or put them in incongruous positions in speeches, which I hope make them funny, simply because they seem slightly out of context."

Clearly, other playwrights have influenced Ayckbourn as well. In an interview with Bernard F. Dukore in *Alan Ayckbourn: A Casebook*, Ayckbourn freely acknowledged his literary muses: "When I started writing I was influenced by practically everything that was ever written. I was in weekly rep. . . . All the plays weren't very good. There were pot boilers. . . . Even the worst of them had moments of great theatricality, which I rather enjoyed. I was born at a very interesting time as a playwright because in my early years there were the very respectable, soon to be rejected before they were reaccepted, playwrights like Nöel Coward, Terence Rattigan, N. C. Hunter, Shaw. There was a whole pre-1950s [set] whom I read and admired a lot. . . . I think I tended, being young, to like what was then the frankly rather dangerous experimental, like Ionesco. Pirandello struck me as being rather interesting — the theatricality. I like Anouilh. Then along came Osborne and Pinter et al. Harold Pinter is one of my first huge major influences." His biographer notes that both Beckett and Pinter made it acceptable to end a play with little-to-no closure. Just as the audience never finds out what happens to Vladimir and Estragon in *Waiting for Godot* or Stanley in *The Birthday Party*, Ayckbourn's plays often end, like life, still in the midst of the process. As Ayckbourn explained to Dukore, " . . . I find it artificial to try to close a play off in that way, to say life stops here. I've always had a feeling that life was going on before the play was written and will continue afterwards, and that there is only a convenient point to interrupt it. . . ."

Several have noted the influence of Jean Anouilh and J. B. Priestly. Like Anouilh, Ayckbourn's plays are well constructed, are difficult to label, and the happy ending does not always ring true nor is it supposed to do so. Pretence is prevalent in both playwrights' works, and they often share a basic theme: incompatible men and women chained together by marriage. Ayckbourn has used variations of Anouilh's *Dinner with the Family* in which characters pretend to be who they are not to other characters, and offstage characters are the focus of onstage action. Kalson suggests that it was Priestly's works that helped Ayckbourn, from the more self-contained south, understand the more in-your-face qualities of the north. Also Priestly's explorations with time shifts within the action and his suggestion of the supernatural, as in *An Inspector Calls*, found their way into some of Ayckbourn's plays, as did Priestly's exploration of the mutability of memory.

TO LONDON VIA THE VICTORIA

Stephen Joseph was looking for a permanent home for his theater-in-the-round. About 150 miles southwest of Scarborough, in the town of Stoke-on-Trent, was the Victoria Theatre. Occupied by a club that featured loud music and gyrating, unclad women, the city revoked its license and agreed to back the endeavor to adapt the Victoria for circle staging. About midway through 1962, the Scarborough Company moved in. Joseph had accepted a teaching post in the theater department at Manchester University, so the job of running the theater fell on Peter Cheeseman. Ayckbourn served as associate director; his principal duties were acting (getting cast in several lead roles) and writing.

At the Victoria, Ayckbourn worked with an actress named Heather Stoney, who later became an important part of his life. He first met Stoney when they performed together in Scarborough shortly before the company moved to the Victoria.

The first season was a financial failure. Cheeseman was forced to make drastic cuts: lowering salaries, releasing company members, and increasing workloads to insure the next season. That 1963 season saw Ayckbourn write, direct, and premiere *Mr. Whatnot*, the play that would be his first to move to London.

Mr. Whatnot marks a major transition in his development. For the first time, he did not write a part in it for himself. This is also the first play of his canon that he allows to be produced today. An homage to Buster Keaton, Harold Lloyd, and silent film, the main character, Mint, never speaks and the props are mimed. The play also reflects Ayckbourn's love of sound effects: he created, recorded, and designed around 150 effects in the play to accompany the mime.

Arriving at a mansion on the wedding day of the lovely ingénue, a working-class piano tuner, Mint, causes bull-in-the-china-shop disasters in the home of the landed gentry. The randy tuner, of course, ends up in bed with the bride by the play's end. When it opened at the Victoria, it was wildly successful with Stoke-on-Trent's working-class audience. It garnered some interest, and producer Peter Bridge decided to produce it in London's West End.

By spring of 1964, some of the Victoria's company had had enough of the low wages and workload and departed. With *Mr. Whatnot* about to open in London, Ayckbourn resigned as well. He also left acting behind. His final role was as Jerry in William Gibson's *Two for the Seesaw*.

When *Mr. Whatnot* was taken to London's West End, it must have seemed like his days of scrambling in the theater were about to pay off. It didn't work out that way. For the first but not the last time, his script, written for the fluid dynamics of an in-the-round production (with sound effects instead of set pieces), was not served well on a proscenium stage with a full set. The critics hated it. Never having received so much bad press, and from London critics at that, Ayckbourn was devastated. When a job presented itself at the BBC Radio in Leeds, he leapt at the chance. By December 1964, he was hired. He, Christine, and the boys moved to Leeds.

WORDS, WORDS, WORDS

At the BBC Radio he was soon in charge of recording radio dramas (having no experience except recording sound effects, limited directing experience, and listening to radio comedies growing up). But he was a quick study, and his sense of humor often saved him.

Until their financial fortunes stabilized, the Ayckbourn's lived in a lower-income, blue-collar neighborhood in Leeds. Philip's bike was stolen by a good friend, and the boy's family saw it as completely normal. This and other events affected Ayckbourn's sense of the damage that an underserved urban landscape can have on its inhabitants. This understanding would later be evidenced in some of his plays.

His time with the BBC Radio also taught him some invaluable lessons about playwriting. He had to read hundreds of submitted scripts and write considered rejections; as such, he learned exactly what did or did not make a good script.

After only a few months at the BBC, Joseph contacted Ayckbourn and asked for a new script for the 1965 summer season, offering some advice as well. Before Ayckbourn wrote a script that broke all the rules (something he had promised to do) he should first write a play that followed the rules. So Ayckbourn set out to write a well-made play. That play not only became his first hit in London but toured America as well.

His initial idea was a story about a young man asking an older man for permission to marry his daughter; only the older man didn't have a daughter. This led to the idea that the young woman was actually the older man's mistress, unbeknownst to both the young man asking for her hand in marriage or the older man's wife, who hasn't a clue who these two young people are. It is a farce of mistaken identities that relies on the particularly British quality of extreme politeness. As Ayckbourn observed, Americans always had trouble with that aspect of British culture; in the United States someone would have blurted out, "Who the hell are you?"

Waiting to the last moment as he usually did, he wrote *Meet My Mother* during a few nights in May and sent it off to Joseph for June rehearsals. Producer Peter Bridge came up to see it, loved it, but wanted a new title. It opened as *Relatively Speaking* in London in 1967. It was hailed as the return of light farce to London. Ayckbourn was declared the West End's version of Neil Simon and the new Nöel Coward. As his biographer, Paul Allen, noted, he even received a telegram from "The Master," Nöel Coward, who congratulated him on a "beautifully constructed and very funny play."

TRANSITIONS

By 1967, while Ayckbourn was still at the BBC, Stephen Joseph was seriously ill with cancer; he died that summer at forty-six years. He lived long enough to see his protégé's play *Relatively Speaking* become a West End success

Ayckbourn was now bereft of both his spiritual father, Joseph, and his biological father, Horace Ayckbourn, who had died ten years earlier, in 1957, of cancer, while the young Ayckbourn was working with Hazel Vincent Wallace's repertory. His mother arrived, and they met for coffee at a pub. She told him that his father had died. He returned to the theater, depressed but silent, keeping his loss to himself.

In 1970, by the time Ayckbourn resigned from the BBC Radio, his marriage was essentially over. Like many marriages, this one did not break apart on a single day. Their youth, early parenthood, his long hours at the theater, the financial stress of low wages, Christine's shifting interest from theater to her sons, and his finding the appeal of other women irresistible resulted in a gradual collapse of the family. By 1963, the marriage was in trouble, but they continued to live together a few more years. When the separation was finally complete, they remained friends, and Christine continued to come to his opening nights.

By 1965, he and Heather Stoney were involved, and he was seeing her whenever he could, although he was still with his wife and sons. Just as the marriage slowly dissolved, his relationship with Stoney had slowly evolved. In 1971, they moved into a home of their own, a duplex in the Hampstead area of London. His boys came to visit, but remained living with their mother until they were off to school. Ayckbourn continued to spend Christmas with his wife and sons, and he and Christine remained married for another thirty years. Clearly, some sort of understanding evolved. When Christine eventually moved from Leeds, it was to a place only a few blocks from Alan and Heather's home, and Christine Ayckbourn began spending Christmas with Alan and Heather Stoney.

Stoney was not only his partner but also the first reader of his scripts. Before the advent of computers, she typed up his scripts as he dictated them (using character voices) from his longhand copy. In a London *Times* article (May 5, 1976) he described the process: "I start dictating. Often things get hopelessly out of hand. Speeches take off, characters take off and they are a series of improvisations. It's quite interesting to work that way. At least everything I've said is spoken once, even if it's only by me and if I can say it, then an actor can say it. If she laughs, we're all right."

EMBARRASSMENT OF RICHES

In 1972, Ayckbourn's spiritual home, now called Scarborough Theatre Trust, became his lifelong home when he became artistic director. He has been known to refer to the theater as his "train set." Ayckbourn devoted himself to directing and running the theater fifty weeks out of the year, getting away for only short periods of time to write. The idea for a play would ruminate in his head for many months as he went about running the theater. The title of the play was announced before a line of dialogue was written. Posters were printed, tickets sold, actors cast. A few days before the first rehearsal, he'd lock himself away and write nearly nonstop, completing the script just before the first rehearsal.

Soon a pattern emerged; he would direct the premiere of his new play in Scarborough's in-the-round space, and it would open the next year or so in London on a proscenium stage (in the early years under someone else's direction, later under his own). Mel Gussow in *The New York Times* (January 28, 1990) observed, "No other playwright of his stature has his own theater. Imagine, if you will, Neil Simon managing a theater in Asbury, N.J., and directing all of his own plays before moving them to Broadway and you might begin to have an idea of Ayckbourn's efforts."

In 1969, the thirty-year-old playwright premiered *How the Other Half Loves* at Scarborough, and in 1970 it opened in London's West End. It was such a success that it ran for two years in London. In 1971, it was the first Ayckbourn play to receive production in New York City.

The play bears the marks of many of his later plays: a clever device that shows off the actors' skills (two sets and two time periods are on one stage simultaneously); put-upon wives (Fiona, Teresa, Mary); and overbearing husbands (Frank, Bob, William), the latter captured in Mary's description of her husband: "It's difficult for him. He's never been wrong before, you see." Like *Relatively Speaking*, the action and much of the humor in *How the Other Half Loves* depends on that quality of British politeness that prevents a character from stating the obvious. That coupled with a manipulation of space and time resulted in a remarkably funny scene of two dinner parties on two different evenings being performed onstage simultaneously. (Ayckbourn often employs meals as the setting for some of his most explosively funny scenes.)

Absurd Person Singular was his next unqualified hit. Here, in Chekhovian fashion, he explored the impact that offstage characters and action have on the on-stage action. Some critics have made a connection to Charles Dickens's *A Christmas Carol*, as each act is set in a different home at Christmas past, Christmas present, and Christmas future. But it isn't a Dickensian tale of moral redemption. As Sidney Howard White observes in his study *Alan Ayckbourn:* "Instead, we have the characteristic Ayckbourn display of middle-class misadventure, in which muddling through becomes a singular English way of life. At times hilarious and at times harrowing, the three acts are really three separate plays loosely held together by the holiday settings and the unique use of the kitchen. The inglorious kitchen becomes the platform for each of the three acts as we watch three married couples celebrate Christmas together." The three couples are representatives of three classes: Sidney and Jane are lower middle class with ambitions, Geoffrey and Eva are middle class and should be rising, Ronald and Marion are upper class and should be solidly on top.

Its celebrated second act finds the despondent and mute Eva utterly determined to commit suicide in various ways as her oblivious guests misunderstand what she is trying to do and "help" her, to hilarious results. When she attempts to gas herself in the oven, the clean-freak Jane pulls her out and proceeds to clean the oven for her. When she tries to hang herself using a laundry line that rips out the ceiling fixture, another guest leaps to her assistance to fix the broken light.

Its third act brings the message of the play home, because it also deals with class inversion. Some see it as a Cassandra play, prophesying the political shift to the right during the Thatcher years with its make-a-profit-at-all-cost philosophy. The act ends with the financially ascendant Sidney making his wife and the other couples dance wildly to his command: "That's it. Dance. Come on. Dance. Dance. Come on. Dance. Dance. Dance. Keep dancing. Dance . . . "

When it came to America, it ran for 592 performances, the longest run for a British import since Nöel Coward's 1941 opening of *Blithe Spirit.* American producers, expecting an Ayckbourn laugh-riot, wanted to switch the decidedly funnier second act with the more disturbing third act, in order to end on a high note. Ayckbourn, understandably, refused.

Ayckbourn's next endeavor was his most daring to date. *The Norman Conquests* is comprised of three plays, which took him eight days to write and premiered in Scarborough in 1973, moving to London's West End in 1974.

The actions of the three plays occur at the same time in three different locations: the dining room (*Table Manners*), the sitting room (*Living Together*), and the garden (*Round and Round the Garden*). It is set in Ayckbourn's favorite playground: middle-class suburbia. He wrote each play to stand alone, as Scarborough vacationers were not likely to spend three nights in the theater. Once again, he explored the world of offstage action but this time by bringing it onstage in the other plays.

Norman's "conquests" are three women: his sister-in-law (Annie), his wife (Ruth), and his brother-in-law's wife (Sarah). Norman often declares his benevolent intentions. To Annie, "I'll make you happy. Don't worry. I'll make you happy." To Ruth, "I want you to be happy. I want everyone to be happy." To Sarah, "I'd very much like to make you happy."

Echoes from his own life can be found throughout the play. Reg, Norman's brother-in-law, is much like the self-indulgent child-man that Ayckbourn's father was. The unseen mom shares his mother's sexual appetite. Reg recalls a childhood experience that actually happened to the playwright: "Do you remember Mother taking us on holiday? . . . When she picked up that sailor? . . . He kept throwing the ball half a mile down the beach. Trying to get us all to run after it." Ayckbourn's mother confirmed that this actually happened when he was a little boy. And Norman's romancing of all the women in the play reflects the playwright himself, who was described as someone who easily laughed women into bed with him.

This trilogy broke the publishing barrier, being the first of his scripts considered literary enough to be published in hard cover. Jack

Tinker in the *Daily Mail* declared that it had "carved a place in the history of British light comedy as indelible as 1066 itself."

In 1975 in London, he had five shows running — the three *Normans*, *Absurd Person Singular*, and *Absent Friends* — making him the first playwright to do so since Nöel Coward in 1925. And to ice that cake, in New York, where they temporarily renamed West 45th Street "Ayckbourn Alley," he had four shows running: the three *Normans* and *Absurd Person Singular*. Now he had the financial means to pursue his art completely as he saw fit.

MOVING TO THE DARK SIDE

Absent Friends, premiering in Scarborough in 1974 and opening in the West End in 1975, is considered a transition play. Ayckbourn himself has acknowledged this. The humor is still there. But issues like the death of relationships and the fantasy of perfect love that can only be preserved through the lens of death are explored more deeply. Critics were expecting the old Ayckbourn, and reviews were mixed. In a *Plays and Players* interview (September 1975), Ayckbourn observed: "I was trying to do something much more low-key. It seemed to me that, if I was going to progress as a dramatist, I must try and get more comedy from character and less from artificially induced situations."

After the epic size of *The Norman Conquests'* three overlapping plays, *Absent Friends* was a simpler, more intimate play, one in which stage time is real time. Ayckbourn has noted that when action time is close to real time, the details of the play gain significance. *Absent Friends* deals with the mutability of memory. It contrasts the pain of miserable relationships that are ongoing to the idealized memory Colin has of his recently deceased fiancée. Ayckbourn created Colin to be seen as a fool, not a positive force. His friends' wretched marriages are thrown in sharp relief as Colin rhapsodizes in apparent happiness about his dead fiancée, a relationship that never had time to go bad, as all the other relationships have. Adultery is central to this play, as it is in many of Ayckbourn's scripts.

> MARGE: Have you been . . . having . . . a love affair with Paul?
> EVELYN: No.
> MARGE: Truthfully?
> EVELYN: I said, no.
> MARGE: Oh. Well. That's all right then. (*Pause*)
> EVELYN: We did it in the back of his car the other afternoon but I wouldn't call that a love affair.

Biographer Paul Allen notes that a member of the original Scarborough audience commented, "If I'd known what I was laughing at while I was watching it, I wouldn't have laughed." As Kalson observed of *Absent Friends*, "It is what Ayckbourn does best — revealing the pain of life through laughter."

In 1975, an artistic marriage, seemingly made in heaven, also proved to be considerably less than ideal. Ayckbourn and Andrew Lloyd Webber joined forces to write a musical. It was based on the comic stories of P. G. Wodehouse concerning the aristocratic Bertie Wooster and his invaluable gentleman's gentleman, Jeeves. Apparently the situation was out of control from the beginning. When *Jeeves* opened in Bristol, they had never had a complete run-through. It ran for over four hours; the union musicians simply walked out at one point. It was cut drastically. Before its London opening, the director was fired, and Ayckbourn took over. Ironically this marked his first London directing experience. The London critics eviscerated it, although a few conceded that Ayckbourn's book and lyrics were wittily fine. It ran for less than a month.

OPENING THE NATIONAL THEATRE

Peter Hall, artistic director of the new National Theatre in London, wanted an Ayckbourn script for the opening, and he agreed that Ayckbourn could co-direct it with him. The script he wrote for Hall was *Bedroom Farce*, writing it over the course of three days and three nights. As was typical, Ayckbourn first directed it on the tiny stage of the Library Theatre in 1975, modifying the acting area into a thrust stage with audience seating on three sides. At the National, it was performed on the wide proscenium stage of the Lyttelton. It marked a return to a laughing comedy with farcical elements and played in London for two and a half years. In 1979, it moved to Broadway with the London cast intact and enjoyed a popular success.

Set in three bedrooms, ironically there is neither adultery nor sex in the play. Ayckbourn employed a filmic technique inspired by D. W. Griffith, crosscutting, whereby shifting rapidly between locations gives the impression that the events are happening at the same time. As described by Benedict Nightingale in *The New York Times* (March 25, 1979): "The play is set in three bedrooms, all of which are seen simultaneously. One is occupied by an elderly couple, who have, says Mr. Ayckbourn, 'given up sex as a bad job and are happiest in bed when they eat sardines together.' In the next room a young husband, bridling at what he touchily assumes to be accusations of sexual inadequacy, is constructing an extremely shaky chest of drawers for his wife. And in the third a 'male chauvinist par excellence' is nursing his bad back. . . . It took him a long time to work out how to link the three bedrooms in some kind of dynamic drama. The solution, obvious once he had thought of it, was to introduce a fourth couple, who spend the night in which the play occurs moving from one house to another, maddening their acquaintances and straining their already troubled marriages."

According to his biographer, Ayckbourn readily admits that he is all four of the men in the play. He, like Nick, had suffered from back strain and was a lousy patient. Just like Trevor, he has a tendency to just blunder through his (and other people's) lives. Malcolm has Ayckbourn's obsession with gadgets (the kind that let you down) and shares a tendency to find humor in crises even after everyone else has stopped laughing. And finally, Ernest's lack of involvement in his son's life echoes the absentee father that Ayckbourn often was.

MOVING TO A NEW SPACE

In 1976, the public library wanted their concert room back (for "cultural purposes"). And the Scarborough company's successes (thanks to Ayckbourn's shore-to-London productions) merited a larger production space. The ground floor of the former Westwood Boys' School became available. Miraculously, after surmounting mountains of bureaucratic red tape, and being blessed with an elderly, renegade architect who started renovations despite no go-ahead from the city, the Scarborough company opened. They presented Ayckbourn's technically challenging *Mr. Whatnot* in October in the new Stephen Joseph Theatre-in-the-Round. The company stayed in the space for twenty-one years.

The first new Ayckbourn play to premiere in the theater was written after Ayckbourn had lived through months of committee hell in getting the new theater opened. In his preface to the play, Ayckbourn described the meetings: "Apparent strong men weaken. Nonentities inherit the floor. Silent men gabble on inarticulately and to no point. Talkative men grow silent and merely emit low indecipherable moans of dissent and agreement. *Ten Times Table* is a study of the committee person."

Ten Times Table was set in the town of Pendon's Swan Hotel Ballroom, during a series of committee meetings as the town tries to establish an annual folk festival. The comic potential of the death-by-small-cuts nature of committee work is fully explored. It is a combination of situation comedy and an agitprop piece as the town Tory and the town Marxist square off. Even though Margaret Thatcher was three years away from being named prime minister, the character of the Conservative socialite sported a Thatcher hairstyle, and the play was clearly about politics as well. Ayckbourn noted in a London *Times* interview

(January 5, 1976): "I'm usually against whichever government is in at the time, simply because it often seems so incompetent. In general, I try to reflect the sort of people I know who are also a bit like this. They don't vote and they have wild prejudices occasionally which are not based on any deep-thought reason. . . . My characters tend to live rather day to day, which I think most people do. They are that great big body in the middle in this country who are don't knows."

EXPANDING HIS RANGE

Ayckbourn continued to explore the possibilities of live performance and stage space. Among his many writing projects, in *Taking Steps* he further explored action taking place in a superimposed space (as he had in *How the Other Half Loves*). He explored the vagaries of chance in multiple-choice plays, including *Intimate Exchanges*. He tried his hand at an adaptation with *A Trip to Scarborough*.

In September 1979, *Taking Steps* premiered, and many welcomed Ayckbourn's return to pure farce. In fact, it is dedicated to that great British farceur, Ben Travers. Since a circle stage does not lend itself to a door-slamming farce, Ayckbourn had to come up with another device. His solution? The ground floor sitting room, the second floor master bedroom, and the third floor attic of a supposedly haunted mansion are all represented simultaneously on the flat stage with stairs rendered on the stage floor. As White described: "Whenever movement is needed from one floor to another, the actors mime the movement in treadmill fashion on the 'flattened steps.'" In an interview in Dukore's *Alan Ayckbourn: A Casebook*, Ayckbourn explained how he made the conceit clear to the audience: "So the first ten minutes of *Taking Steps* has to do with telling people the geography of the house. I made sure a man went up to the attic with a suitcase and came down again, he talked, and then he went downstairs. And by the end, where Elizabeth is jumping on the ceiling and the men are standing physically right next to her, plaster from above falls on them. The audience laughs although the whole thing is nonsense." Another example is when the character of Roland is explaining to Tristram, on the "first floor," that the house was once a brothel and is rumored to be haunted by a murdered prostitute. At this point, a female character, fumbling her way to the attic, literally walks between them but is "unseen" because she is on another floor, although her footsteps heard "overhead" rattle Tristram, who fears it is the ghost.

It was wildly successful in Scarborough, and often the "Ayckbourn roar" was heard. The proscenium staging in London (1980) was not successful, as the floor was not visible. In *The Crafty Art of Playmaking*, Ayckbourn observed that he felt that *How the Other Half Loves* and *Taking Steps* work far better in the round because the floor is visible to the audience. The "Ayckbourn roar" in Scarborough became near silence in the West End. The rumors started — Ayckbourn was no longer the writer he used to be.

Ayckbourn continued to explore. Believing that the course of one's life is often charted by chance, he wrote his first multiple-choice play, *Sisterly Feelings*, in which a coin toss and a decision to go or stay results in the play's action going in different directions. In many ways, this play prepared him to write the mother of all multiple-choice plays, *Intimate Exchanges.*

For the 1982 summer season, Ayckbourn let all but two of his actors off. The two remaining actors, Robin Herford and Lavinia Bertram, were in for the ride of their professional lives, playing ten characters in eight plays with sixteen possible endings. Writing with them in mind, he gave each actor a character they could readily identify with, one that was a fun-to-play caricature, one that would stretch them as actors, as well as a couple of others. The script ran to over four hundred pages and presented a formidable memorization challenge for the actors, as well as a logistical nightmare to get all versions adequately rehearsed.

Two of the central characters, an alcoholic headmaster, Toby, and his anxious wife, Celia, were inspired by the couple who ran Ayckbourn's old school, Wisborough Lodge.

A breakdown only begins to suggest the complexities of this script. Scene One, "How it Began," has two possible endings: a character does or does not smoke a cigarette, leading to two different scenes, "A Gardener Calls" and "A Visit from a Friend." Each of these scenes has two possible endings, leading to four possible scenes that occur five days later. Each of these four scenes has alternate endings, leading to eight possible scenes that occur five weeks later. And, of course, each of these scenes has two possible outcomes, leading to sixteen possible epilogues that occur five years later. A chart was hung in the lobby to indicate which track the performance would take each evening. In the final two weeks of the run, to celebrate this great achievement, all eight plays with their sixteen endings were run back to back.

With two actors playing all of the characters, the challenges were multiplied. Sometimes they exited as one character and spoke as another character as soon as they got offstage. In one scene, the single actress plays two female characters having a fight behind a curtain. Each actor would exit as one character and enter moments later as a completely different character and from a different entrance location, necessitating a change of costume and sometimes makeup as well. Allen notes that Herford, who was terrified of memorizing so much material, recalled, "You knew that behind you was this huge body of work. You've seen Toby at his wildest and you've seen him at his most pathetic and you can call on both of those to play whatever's in front of you at the moment. It was almost an orgy of acting."

After playing in the round at Scarborough, *Intimate Exchanges*, with its cast and invaluable dresser, transferred to a proscenium stage in London. All in all, on and off, the play ran until February 1985. In 1993, the famous French New Wave cinema director Alain Resnais (*Hiroshima Mon Amour*) directed a film version of *Intimate Exchanges* in two parts: *Fumer/Non Fumer* (*Smoking/Nonsmoking*).

For his 1982 Christmas offering, Ayckbourn decided to try his hand at writing an adaptation. The result was *A Trip to Scarborough*, an adaptation of Richard Brinsley Sheridan's 1777 play of the same name. Ayckbourn sets it in three different time periods: 1800, 1942, and the present. The fact that the same stories of love occur during each time period is emphasized in a costume ball that gradually results in everyone running around in eighteenth-century garb. He went on to write other adaptations over the course of his career: *Tons of Money* (1986), based on one of the original "Aldwych farces"; *Wolf at the Door* (1989), based on Henry Becque's *Les Corbeaux;* and *The Forest* (1999), based on Alexander Ostrovsky's play of the same name.

GETTING POLITICAL AND PESSIMISTIC

Ayckbourn, as a rule, seems generally disgusted with politics. In his *The Crafty Art of Playmaking*, he stated, "Once you allow a political vacuum to occur through apathy, you invite extremism. Seeking a quiet, selfish life, many are content to follow anyone who purports to know what they're doing and where we should all be going. Witness the last few decades of British politics." The Thatcher years provoked the playwright, who had pretty much avoided overtly political plays, to speak out. And he did it with his marvelous infusion of humor. This is most appropriate for the man whom many call the modern Molière. As Molière himself stated concerning his controversial *Tartuffe*: "To expose vices to everyone's laughter is to deal them a mighty blow. People easily endure reproofs, but they cannot at all endure being made fun of. People have no objection to being considered wicked, but they are not willing to be considered ridiculous." In *Way Upstream* Ayckbourn calls on those living quiet and selfish lives to stand up to the tyranny of self-interest and evil.

In 1979 Margaret Thatcher and the Conservative Party had ushered in the most right-wing government in over forty years due to widespread frustration with the trade unions. A faction of the outgoing Labour Party broke away and formed the new Social Democratic Party. There was incredible animosity on all sides. Hate was in the air.

At the time of *Way Upstream*, which premiered in Scarborough in 1981, Ayckbourn had only voted once in his life, and then only because a friend was running. This reflects his deep distrust of politicians and his refusal to align with any party, since he believed they're all crooked. *Way Upstream* is an examination of the personal — what happens when one person tried to force others into a lock step; it echoes Ayckbourn's belief that governments often try the same thing. His biographer, who is also a theater critic, noted: "Only after the performance did we start to realize that Ayckbourn had been *far* more adventurous in terms of his content: at the start of the most selfish, materialistic and confrontational decade in living memory he had written about good and evil, a moral fable."

Way Upstream could not have found a better visual metaphor for the sense that the ground was shifting beneath the very foundation of British society — that of a boat on troubled waters. Ayckbourn had long been intrigued with the idea of setting a play on water, and as the theater had concrete floors, he knew that he could get away with it. A swimming pool company recommended a bolted wooden frame and a polystyrene liner, and a local ship builder was contracted to build a cabin cruiser with a flat bottom.

The action starts at Pendon Bridge in the Home Counties and goes down the River Orb to Armageddon Bridge. As the names suggest, the play moves from realism to near-allegory. The program declared it was "a tale of mutiny and piracy aboard a cabin cruiser on a sleepy English river." The boat cruised under bridges, weighed anchor, and tied up at a wooden jetty beside a private island.

The series of misadventures that occurred also had roots in Ayckbourn's past. As he related to Kalson: "I did the maddest thing, that no one in his right mind should do, shortly after I was married. I went up a river with my in-laws, my wife and my mother. On the first day my mother fell off the side of the boat and cracked her ribs and had to lie in the front cabin for the whole trip just moaning quietly and looking out the porthole on one elbow, saying, 'No, no, I'll just enjoy the scenery.' And my father-in-law and I decided we weren't going to get on very well and just screamed at each other. A lot of what happens in the play happened to us, including running aground three times. . . . An extraordinary microcosm exists on boats."

When it moved to the National's Lyttelton Theatre in 1982, a proscenium space with Ayckbourn directing, disaster awaited. The show was over-designed, the tank cracked, and gallons of water poured down into the electrical control room. Finally Ayckbourn made the hard call; it would be performed without water. Several previews had to be cancelled — three times after the audience had already arrived. Sadly, by the time it opened, it was already a laughing stock, with one critic showing up in Wellington boots.

In addition to getting more political, Ayckbourn was also getting more pessimistic, although anyone paying attention should have seen *Woman in Mind* coming. Back in 1976 he wrote *Just Between Ourselves*, which possesses an ending that chilled audiences to the bone (and made many resentful that they were not getting an Ayckbourn laugh riot). What in previous plays had been the hilarity of watching men drive women mad in this play actually becomes the portrait of a woman taking the long fall to emotional collapse over the course of four birthdays being "celebrated." In his preface to the play, he described Vera as a wife who "suffers from a conventional upbringing that has taught her that the odds of her being wrong and her husband right are high. Slowly the last vestiges of self-confidence are drained out of her."

With *Woman in Mind*, which premiered in Scarborough in 1985, he would write one of his most pessimistic plays to date. Like Vera in *Just Between Ourselves*, the audience watches Susan, an unhappy wife, have a nervous breakdown, but in *Woman in Mind*, the audience is seeing the collapse of reality through Susan's eyes as she experiences it. After knocking herself out with a lawn rake, she can't understand what her doctor says. She hears, "Squeezy, cow, squeezy," when he is actually saying, "Easy, now easy." But after the language problems clear up, it becomes clear that she is seeing the world around her in an idealized form, including a seemingly perfect family. But the dream becomes a nightmare when her dream family and her real family merge into hellish realms. As the play ends, an ambulance's blue lights flash as Susan's language descends into gibberish. Her last words echo *Hamlet:* "December bee? December bee" — "Remember me."

Ayckbourn's great sympathy for women descending into marriage-induced breakdowns connects to his own mother, who experienced a mental collapse shortly after the young Alan had graduated from school. He helped her out of the marriage and into a job and an apartment. Of *Woman in Mind*, he told his biographer: "Obviously there was a tiny element of my mother in there although, looking at it now, I know there were faults on both sides. But she did have a marriage with a man she felt didn't appreciate her." Another influence was Oliver Sacks' study of neurological injuries, *The Man Who Mistook His Wife for a Hat*. Years later, in 1998, Ayckbourn noted that *A Doll's House* may have also been a subconscious influence. Indeed, one can hear Nora in Susan's lines: "I used to be a wife. I used to be a mother. And I loved it."

AN OFFER HE COULDN'T REFUSE

In 1986, Peter Hall offered Ayckbourn the direction of his own company at the National Theatre. It was the one thing that could pull him away from Scarborough. Most people assumed he would never return. He took many of his regular actors with him, finally having the opportunity to show London what his Scarborough company could do. There he directed *Tons of Money*, his adaptation previously performed in Scarborough in 1986. And he showed off his serious directing prowess with Arthur Miller's *A View from a Bridge*, winning the Laurence Olivier Award for Best Director.

The same month *A View from a Bridge* opened, February 1987, the queen invested him with the Companion of the Order of the

British Empire. Both she and the queen mother were known to enjoy his comedies, although not his darker plays.

On May 21, 1987, he premiered a new script, *A Small Family Business*, which was written for the daunting proscenium stage of the Olivier, the National's largest space. Peter Hall had to approve the play first. As such, it was the first play Ayckbourn finished well in advance of rehearsals. Kalson notes that just as Priestly's play *An Inspector Calls* was meant to show up the social ills that led to the two world wars, Ayckbourn's *A Small Family Business* shows up the disastrous results of Margaret Thatcher's policies on English middle-class business and morals. Ayckbourn has confirmed that *A Small Family Business* expressed his feelings about Thatcher's policies and what England had become during her seven years in office. The family of *A Small Family Business* reflected a society where greed and the accumulation of wealth were political virtues, where the ends always justified the means, as well as a government and business climate where the assent of the populace was never solicited. In it, a man, Jack McCracken, determined to be ethical himself, demands ethical behavior from his company and family. However, step-by-step, compromise-by-compromise, he is gradually overcome by dirty money, drugs, and murder.

In *The Crafty Art of Playmaking*, Ayckbourn explained that he was trying to find "the darkness that lurked behind the cheery family exterior. (It's actually a comedy about greed, blackmail, adultery, prostitution, organized crime, sexual deviation, murder and teenage death through drug addition — though we never billed it as that!)" The play ends as the formally upright Jack makes a toast to the family business (which has now become "the family" Mafia style), as his youngest daughter sits staring into space, stoned out on the drugs that her family will now sell. It quickly took in one million pounds at the box office, an audience attendance record.

In 1988 he returned to Scarborough to again take up the reins as artistic director. He was home for good.

SUFFER THE LITTLE CHILDREN

Needing to build up a children's audience for Scarborough's 1988 Christmas season, and rightly believing that top playwrights should be writing plays for the next generation of audiences, he began writing family and children's plays. Except for three plays written in the 60s, this marked a new avenue of exploration for him, one that opened the world of his plays to more fantastical, more film-like approaches. In the Dukore interview, Ayckbourn discussed the terror of writing for children: "It's very frightening because they are far and away, as everyone knows, the most demanding and critical and short-patiented of audiences. An adult audience will give you ten, fifteen minutes. They'll say, 'Well, give it time to get going.' Kids'll give you about a half a minute. Then they turn and talk to their friends. All the elements are frightening and have to come together very sharply: character, narrative, brevity, action are terribly important, at the same time trying to keep some semblance of dramatic shape to it."

A brief sampling serves to demonstrate the remarkable range of these scripts. Ayckbourn told Dukore that *Mr. A's Amazing Maze Plays* was "a sort of *Intimate Exchanges* gone mad." Young Suzy's father has disappeared in a balloon (wearing the flying cap and goggles Ayckbourn remembers his father wearing). She must outwit the villainous Mr. Accousticus, who steals sounds and voices. As young Suzy tries to expose the sound stealer before her mother marries him, the audience gets to choose which of the twenty-five rooms in Mr. Accousticus's mansion she will search. *This Is Where We Came In*, employing music to help tell the story, shows a clear connection to Pirandello's *Six Characters in Search of an Author*. Characters are forced to repeatedly act out stories told by three elderly tellers-of-tales. Eventually, one character frees them from this anarchy, and they are now free to tell their own stories. *Whenever*, a time-traveling musical written with composer Denis King, takes its inspiration from science fiction writers, as well as Frank L. Baum's *Wizard of Oz*. An unhappy orphan goes on a journey to return home and meets on her journey a soldier, an android, and a furry beast.

The otherwise happy ending is tempered when her friend the soldier announces he is traveling to 1914 to join a "war that will put a stop to all wars." While Ayckbourn gives his family audiences a happy ending, he never talks down to youth. Reality always stands hand in hand with fiction. It was a critical and popular success and is considered by many to be one of his best family plays. In his collection of children's plays, the play *Orvin, Champion of Champions* was written for the young cast of the National Youth Music Theatre and is a medieval adventure story by way of a social comedy. *The Ten Magic Bridges*, *Miranda's Magic Mirror*, and *The Girl Who Lost Her Voice* are each a children's play series inspired by the Saturday morning film series of his childhood. On consecutive weekend mornings, children were entertained by a scene that included adventure, audience interaction, a song, and a cliffhanger ending to bring them back the next Saturday.

In an article in the *Evening Standard* (March 8, 1991), Ayckbourn observed that many mistakenly believe that "the only things that will attract children are the very loud and the very very crude, mostly in terms of wide slapstick. Children can take fear, they can take excitement, they can take tension, they can take sorrow. They can take Bambi's mother dying. One hopes that the spectrum of emotion isn't filtered out and you don't just get custard being poured over people, although I think a bit of custard, even in adult plays, is fine." He adds that while despair is acceptable in adult plays, one needs to end plays for children on a hopeful note. As an example, *Invisible Friends* was, in many ways, a kid-friendly version of *Woman in Mind*, his adult play about a woman who hallucinates new family members. But apropos of the hopes he wants to instill in his youngest audience members, little Lucy realizes that she must defy her invisible friend and live in the real world. *Woman in Mind* ends in horror, *Invisible Friends* in family love.

SETTLING IN AT SCARBOROUGH

After returning to Scarborough, the plays he wrote continued to challenge audience's expectations. As he stated in *The New York Times* (January 28, 1990): "It used to be said that the audience would laugh at my plays as the curtain left the deck. Now there's a slight wariness because they're not quite sure which way we're going to take them. They know my plays are mine fields." The *Revengers' Comedies* (1989) was one such mine-field.

Written as a fiftieth-birthday present to himself, it's a two-part play with a total running time of six hours. The audience must see both parts and in the right order for it to make sense. Part One is wonderfully funny, Part Two is unsettling. As he had in *Bedroom Farce*, he again adapted D. W. Griffith's crosscutting for the stage to cut between the action in the city and the action in the country.

Premiering in 1989 in Scarborough, it was inspired by the revenge tragedies of Elizabethan/Jacobean England and Alfred Hitchcock's 1951 *Strangers on a Train*. As such there are deaths right-and-left, most intentional, all amusing. In *Revengers' Comedies*, a man and a woman meet on a foggy bridge intent on committing suicide. Instead they concoct a plan to be the instrument of the other's vengeance. Henry Bell is one of Ayckbourn's hopeless males who wreck havoc nonetheless. Karen Knightly, on the other hand, is alarmingly efficient and without a moral center. Karen, to a large extent, reflects Ayckbourn's view that society's me-first attitude encourages people to make up rules to their own advantage.

Henry goes to the country to get revenge on the man who dumped Karen, and in the process finds love. Karen goes to the city to get revenge on the company that dumped Henry and ends up unscrupulously clawing her way to the top. When Karen learns that Henry is marrying the very woman she wanted killed, the two meet again on the bridge, and she takes vengeance on him: "Go home to your cozy little country cottage with your pigs and your cows and your hideous children. You'll never be free of me. You'll remember me with guilt in your hearts for ever. For ever . . . Ever . . . Henry Bell!! She jumps to her death screaming "Reve-e-e-e-n-n-g-e!"

Kalson identifies a recurring Ayckbourn theme in *Revengers' Comedies*: "that sane men and women permit others to encroach on their personal affairs and daily lives, that a nation's citizens complacently sit by while a chosen few — the self-chosen few — dictate actions of earthshaking proportions. . . ." He goes on to comment that ". . . Ayckbourn confidently uses caricature that stops just short of expressionism to populate a play about a nation too far off course ever to recover its sanity, humanity, and morality."

THE CRAFTY ART

Following in the footsteps of Stephen Sondheim and Ian McKellan, in 1992 he was named the Cameron Mackintosh Visiting Professor of Contemporary Theatre at the University of Oxford. He offered two courses: playwriting and directing. His students ranged from undergraduates to senior faculty to local housewives. Ten years later, Ayckbourn published *The Crafty Art of Playmaking*, a marvelous text on playwriting and directing, complete with 101 "Obvious Rules" and superb examples from his own scripts and directing experience.

The volume offers particular insight into how Ayckbourn can write a play in only a few days. By the time he actually puts the script on paper, all that is left is the dialogue. His "Obvious Rule No. 23" is "You can't spend too much time on this first phase. It can take at least a year." Phase one involves coming up with an idea and letting it ruminate (preferably while puttering in the garden). He elaborates in considerable detail on the practical considerations of crafting the narrative, time, location, and characters. He emphasizes that these four must be in place before a word of dialogue is written. As his biographer observed, "Although the proportion of his life spent actually writing plays is very short, there is a part of him always at work on one. . . . Far from being a kind of computer, as people sometimes guess, his mind is like an Aladdin's Cave where the treasures are characters, experiences, emotions of unknown provenance; they have never been catalogued or put in order." He has described his writing as a form of blessed insanity. In *The New York Times* (January 28, 1990), he stated that writing was like having "a reasonably well controlled multiple personality." His greatest fear is of being cured.

BE CAREFUL WHAT YOU ASK FOR

The company outgrew its space in the old Westwood school, just as it had outgrown the library. In 1990, Ayckbourn and several of the theater's wealthiest board members acquired the lease of the Odeon cinema. It seemed a worthy location to realize Stephen Joseph's dream of a permanent theater-in-the-round. Until the new theater opened in 1996, as he pursued his other artistic aims, a part of his brain and time was spent making this come about. It was a tortuous process involving even more bureaucratic wrangling than the last time the company had moved.

The Odeon cinema is a 1930s art deco building. It was converted at the cost of over five million pounds and named the Stephen Joseph Theatre. It opened on May 1, 1996 (the theater license arriving from the town hall two hours before the first performance). The renovation included two theaters: The Round (the main circle stage), designed as close as possible to Stephen Joseph's plans, and The McCarthy (a smaller proscenium space).

Such an eventful and long-awaited opening deserved something special for the first performance, and the new theater got it when Ayckbourn and Andrew Lloyd Webber again joined forces to salvage their failure of over twenty years before. The result was *By Jeeves*.

MUSIC MAN

Despite the disaster of *Jeeves*, Ayckbourn had continued to write a fair share of musicals and revues, including *Suburban Strains* (1980), *Making Tracks* (1981), and *Dreams of a Summer House* (1992).

On May 1, 1996, a scaled-down revision of *Jeeves* opened in The Round. Now retitled *By Jeeves*, Ayckbourn and Andrew Lloyd Webber reduced the 1975 cast of twenty-one to ten; a full orchestra became a five-piece band; Webber provided new songs (retaining only three from the original), and Ayckbourn completely rewrote the book. It was well received by audience and critics and moved to a successful West End run. In 1996, under Ayckbourn's direction, *By Jeeves* began a series of productions in various locations in North America. A production from Pittsburg was scheduled to open on Broadway when the planes hit the towers on September 11, 2001. Given the emotional climate in New York, the Broadway producers pulled their funding. But Andrew Lloyd Webber, feeling that a British presence on Broadway would show England's support, raised the funds himself. It opened on October 28, 2001, running for three months in a city badly shaken by the terrorist attacks.

A KNIGHTHOOD, A DIVORCE, A MARRIAGE, A DEATH

On February 11, 1997, Queen Elizabeth II knighted him "for services to the theatre." Heather Stoney and his sons attended the ceremony.

Despite the fact that Alan and Heather Stoney had been a couple for many years, Ayckbourn and Christine were still married. Most people simply assumed that he and Stoney were husband and wife. Thus it came as a surprise in 1997 when it was announced that he and Christine were divorcing. She had offered him a divorce on several occasions, but as he did not think he would ever marry again, he saw no need. But after the knighthood, as Stoney explained to Paul Allen, "I suppose you get to a certain age and it starts to seem silly not to tidy things up." The divorce was finalized by May 1997. With only two friends as witnesses, he and Heather Stoney got married in September at a local register office.

In February 1999, he was already in bed when he was notified at 10:30 PM of his mother's death. As is his nature, his reaction, according to his biographer, was "barely noticeable." As many have observed of Ayckbourn, he wears his emotions very close. At her funeral in Scarborough, Ayckbourn wrote a prose ode to his mother: sad, outrageous, and true — a litany of the cockeyed life he led with her. There were the men (husbands, live-ins, and "uncles"), there were the cigarettes (and some fires), there was the working woman (pounding away on her typewriter). Then there was the mentally absent mom (using salt instead of sugar in a birthday cake or putting two newborn puppies in the oven to warm and then forgetting about them), and there was the woman scorned (furiously calling his father a "bastard" as she threw his framed photograph at her son). There was the woman who, he concluded, "gave me far more complexes, hang-ups, phobias, prejudices, inspirations and self-insights than any writer has a right to expect from a parent . . . to her, many thanks, much love and farewell." She died just shy of her ninety-third birthday.

BACK TO THE NATIONAL, TURNING HIS BACK ON THE WEST END

In 2000, Ayckbourn returned to the National Theatre with two plays, *House* and *Garden*. As in *Absurd Person Singular* and *Norman Conquests*, these plays deal with offstage action. But *House* and *Garden* share a single narrative and are performed simultaneously in two theaters sharing the same cast.

In April 1999, Ayckbourn turned sixty and treated himself to these two plays, knowing that the close proximity of his two new stages would allow their synchronized performance. *House* was performed in the proscenium space and *Garden* in the circle space. Two stage managers were in constant contact with each other, making sure the two plays stayed in sync. For example, when a character announces in the house that he's taking the dog for a walk, he exits the stage and a few moments later turns up on the other stage's garden calling, "Come along, boy!" Ayckbourn never expected it to be performed anywhere except Scarborough due to the production demands. But the artistic director at the National Theatre, Trevor Nunn, offered Ayckbourn the two proscenium spaces at the National to restage the plays in London, where they opened August 9, 2000. Because the distance between these theaters was further than in Scarborough, Ayckbourn came up with the "Emergency Dog," a character's dog that would bark (offstage) and let the actors on stage know there was going to be a late entrance, thus allowing the delivery of some additional dialogue to cover the gap. *House* and *Garden* were the talk of theater season. They were a critical and popular success. Charles Spencer of the *Daily Telegraph* proclaimed that Ayckbourn was "back at the very top of his form."

House and *Garden* riffs on the idea that just because a person may be a central character in the life of some, he or she is a peripheral character to others. So the main characters in one play were often on the fringes of the other play. These plays also marked a return to one of his (and his audiences') favorite subjects, the lives of frustrated couples (a woman is even driven mad). Set in the spatial country home of Teddy and Trish Platt, Trish is so fed up with her husband's affairs that she simply pretends he's not in the room anymore.

TRISH: No, I'm sorry, Gavin, I can't find Teddy anywhere. Don't know where he's gone. (*Teddy laughs. Gavin laughs a little forcedly.*) . . . Now, we've just heard that their car's turned into the village, so Madame Cadeau plus her driver should be with us any minute. Lucille Cadeau. I don't know if you've heard of her. She's a French film star.

TEDDY: Yes, I've just told him, Trish . . .

TRISH: Have you heard of her, at all?

GAVIN: I hadn't, but —

TEDDY: I've told him, she's coming to open our fête . . .

TRISH: She's here to open our garden fête this afternoon.

In the wooing of Teddy to join politics, Ayckbourn's general disgust and mistrust of all things political was also on display. Tony Blair's Labour government was not seen as a significant improvement, especially the cozy relationship between the land-owning gentry and New Toryism (demanding social justice while simultaneously upholding high standards of living for the old money and newly rich). New Labour had enjoyed a huge success in the General Election of 1997, but Ayckbourn commented that England had merely elected a PR firm to run the government.

Ayckbourn's return to the National was shortly followed by his departure from the West End beginning when he moved *Damsels in Distress*, a trilogy, to the West End's Duchess Theatre.

Back in Scarborough, after a period of casting individual shows, *Damsels in Distress* returned the theater to its repertory roots. The three unconnected plays (*GamePlan*, *FlatSpin*, *RolePlay*) were written to be performed by the same cast on the same set, opening a few weeks apart in 2001.

These were the first plays he had written for specific actors since *Intimate Exchanges*. In the preface to *Damsels in Distress*, Ayckbourn explained: ". . . I began to yearn, once again, for a permanent acting company which during the sixties, seventies and early eighties were the mainstay of the Theatre in Scarborough. . . . The moment when a group of individual (sometimes highly individual) actors through familiarity, growing confidence and trust in each other forms that most unique of all theatrical achievements — a shared 'corporate' identity. The individuality remains — but the sum of the separate parts has generated something greater and stronger."

Opening on the West End in September 2002, London reviews favored *RolePlay*, so the producer drastically reduced the performances of *GamePlan* and *FlatSpin*. Feeling betrayed, Ayckbourn boycotted the West End. In 2007 he conditionally lifted the boycott and allowed a revival of his 1972 classic, *Absurd Person Singular*: revivals yes, but no new scripts. Despite calls from critics that the West End should book his new plays, he held firm. Instead his new plays toured the provinces under his own terms.

ON HIS OWN TERMS IN SCARBOROUGH

Exploring new territory in a quite cinematic approach, *Private Fears in Public Places* premiered in 2004 in The Round, moved to London's only permanent theater-in-the-round, and transferred with the same cast to the Brits Off-Broadway Festival in New York. While it encountered lukewarm reviews in England, in America it was a critical and popular hit. In 2006, French director Alain Resnais (who had directed the film adaptation of *Intimate Exchanges*) adapted it into the acclaimed film *Coeurs* (*Hearts*).

Ayckbourn confirmed that it was inspired by his love of film; in fact, it is meant to be a film on stage. Several interlocking stories are told in fifty-four scenes with numerous location changes, played without intermission with quick crosscutting between scenes. It is also one of his darkest plays and examines the lives of "thirty-somethings" at the beginning of the twenty-first century. Charles Isherwood of *The New York Times*, described it: "A minor-key comedy about six Londoners leading lives of quiet desperation, it is rueful, funny, touching and altogether wonderful . . . . A delicate play with the transparent texture of a piece of chamber music, it comprises of dozens of brief scenes, most with no obvious comic payoff. Some are wordless tableaus: a woman sitting alone in a café, shrinking sadly into a cappuccino cup, a man moored in an armchair before a flickering television screen, lost in wonder at what he sees before him. . . . Sir Alan never allows his humor to warp the humanity of his characters. . . . Each struggles with the problem of how and when secret anxieties and hopes should be divulged to friends, lovers and strangers, what must be risked to forge the connections that sustain life and give it richness."

LIFE INTERRUPTED (BUT NOT FOR LONG)

On February 21, 2006, Ayckbourn visited his osteopath. While there, he suffered a stroke. He described the experience in *The Independent* (August 24, 2008): "The first couple of weeks, lying there in the hospital, taking stock of my situation, I came round with the thought, 'My God, I'm playless.' I cannot imagine living without a play in me. Slowly, though, they started to arrive, and everything else, mobility and so on, came back quite quickly. But I thought the writing would be easier to get back to than the directing and in fact the opposite has been the case. I've found I'm like a plant in water when I'm out of a rehearsal room. I wilt. I start thinking I'm near death. I use the energy of a cast to swing round the sun, like a rocket uses gravity. The writing took longer and was much more difficult, oddly. You're on your own." Six months later he was back in the rehearsal room with *If I Were You*, even though his doctor told him it was too soon.

He had written *If I Were You* before his stroke, so the question loomed, could he still write or had the stroke permanently taken his plays from him. The question was answered when he wrote and directed *Life and Beth*. Premiering on July 22, 2008, in The Round, it was the third of his so-called ghost plays. Combining the casts from two previous ghost plays, it was performed in repertory with *Haunting Julia* and *Snake in the Grass* in a 2008 summer season called *Things That Go Bump*.

In *Life and Beth*, Beth's husband, Gordon, has died after thirty-three years of marriage, and the family gathers for a wretched Christmas. Michael Billington in *The Guardian* (July 23, 2008) described the play as "full of ghosts: not just spooks, but haunting echoes of themes that have animated his work over 40 years." He goes on to explain "it feels both like a summing-up and a wise, humane, funny play about the inevitability of death and the continuity of life. He concludes with a marvelous summation of the play's theme: "What makes the play both comic and touching is Ayckbourn's indignant sympathy for oppressed women. You realize that Beth was cowed by the appalling Gordon, and when his son says 'most of the women I've been out with start crying sooner or later', you get an instant image of a grisly inheritance. Few dramatists in history have painted a more devastating picture of the emotional damage wrought by bullying men. [The character of] the stoic Beth, however, shows that they can triumph, and there is priceless support from . . . a beaming cleric who croons that you should 'accentuate the positive, eliminate the negative', which, in the end, is roughly the message of Ayckbourn's life-affirming ghost story."

After his stroke, despite his return to directing and writing, Ayckbourn realized that he needed to cut back on his responsibilities. As such, after nearly forty years as artistic director, Ayckbourn announced that he would step down, but would continue to write and direct the premieres of his plays.

Sir Alan Ayckbourn is a playwright who has made a career of finding humor in the horrifying: man's inhumanity to woman, woman's inhumanity to man, and humanity's inhumanity to the world. In his interview with Dukore in *Alan Ayckbourn: A Casebook*, he observed, "I once said that comedy is tragedy interrupted. What I meant was, sometimes it depends where you cut the cord and say, 'Well, we'd better finish the story here, folks. If you carry it for another ten minutes the husband will not be living happily ever after with his wife. He'll be strangling her. So let's quit while the story is still fairly happy." For all of our sakes, let's hope his life continues to be tragedy interrupted so that the world's stages can continue to be edified and entertained by this jester with a humanist's heart.

DRAMATIC MOMENTS

from the Major Plays

These short excerpts are from the playwright's major plays. They give a taste of the work of the playwright. Each has a short introduction in brackets that helps the reader understand the context of the excerpt. The excerpts, which are in chronological order, illustrate the main themes mentioned in the In an Hour essay.

from **Absurd Person Singular** (1972)

CHARACTERS

Eva

Geoffrey

Jane

[Act Two, shortly after the beginning. Geoffrey and Eva Jackson are in the kitchen of their fourth-floor flat. As Geoffrey tries to stave off disaster, Eva's attempts at suicide are blithely misunderstood by their guests. As with all of Ayckbourn's scripts, for the reader to begin to understand the effectiveness of his comedy, the action and characters must be envisioned.]

(Geoffrey returns with a couple of old coffee cups which he puts in the sink.)

GEOFFREY: That room is like a very untidy cesspit. (*He finds a dishcloth.*) One quick drink that's all they're getting. Then it's happy Christmas and out they bloody well go.

(Geoffrey goes out again. He takes with him the dishcloth. Eva opens her notepad and continues with her note. Geoffrey returns. He still has the cloth. In the other hand he has a pile of bits of broken dog biscuit.)

GEOFFREY: Half-chewed biscuit. Why does he only chew half of them, can you tell me that? (*He deposits the bits in the waste bin. He is about to exit again, then pauses.*) Eva? Eva — I'm being very patient. Very patient indeed. But in a minute I really do believe I'm going to lose my temper. And we know what happens then, don't we? I will take a swing at you and then you will feel hard done and, by way of reprisal, will systematically go round and smash everything in the flat. And come tomorrow breakfast time, there will be the familiar sight of the three of us, you, me and George, trying to eat our meals off our one surviving plate. Now, Eva, *please . . .*

(The doorbell rings. George starts barking.)

GEOFFREY: Oh, my God. Here's the first of them. (*Calling.*) George. Now, Eva, go to bed now, please. Don't make things any more embarrassing. (*As he goes out.*) George, will you be quiet.

(Geoffrey goes out. The door closes. Silence. Eva opens her notepad, finishes her note and tears it out. She pushes the clutter on the table to one side slightly. She goes to a drawer and produces a kitchen knife. She returns to the table and pins the note forcibly to it with the knife. She goes to the window. Geoffrey returns. Barking and chattering are heard in the background — two voices. Eva stands motionless, looking out.)

GEOFFREY: (*Calling back.*) He's all right. He's quite harmless. Bark's worse than his bite. (*He closes the door.*) It would be the bloody Hopcrofts, wouldn't it? Didn't think they'd miss out. And that lift's broken down, would you believe it? (*Finding a bottle opener in a drawer.*) Every Christmas. Every Christmas, isn't it? Eva, come on, love, for heaven's sake. (*Geoffrey goes out, closing the door.*)

(Eva opens the window. She inhales the cold fresh air. After a second, she climbs uncertainly onto the window ledge. She stands giddily, staring down and clutching onto the frame. The door opens, chatter, Geoffrey returns, carrying a glass. Calling behind him.)

GEOFFREY: I'll get a clean one, I'm terribly sorry. I'm afraid the cook's on holiday. (*He laughs. The Hopcroft's laughter is heard. Geoffrey closes the door.*) Don't think we can have washed these glasses since the last party. This one certainly didn't pass the Jane Hopcroft Good Housekeeping Test, anyway. (*He takes a dishcloth from the sink and wipes the glass rather casually.*) I sometimes think that woman must spend . . . Eva! What are you doing?

(Eva, who is feeling sick with vertigo, moans.)

GEOFFREY: Eva! Eva — that's a good girl. Down. Come down — come down — that's a good girl — down. Come on . . . (*He reaches Eva.*) That's it. Easy. Come on, I've got you. Down you come. That's it.

(*He eases Eva gently back into the room. She stands limply. He guides her inert body to a chair.*)

GEOFFREY: Come on, sit down here. That's it. Darling, darling, what were you trying to do? What on earth made you want to . . . ? What *was* the point of that, what were you trying to prove? I mean . . . (*He sees the note and the knife for the first time.*) What on earth's this? (*He reads it.*) Oh, no. Eva, you mustn't think of . . . I mean, what do you mean, a burden to everyone? Who said you were a burden? I never said you were a burden . . .

(*During the above, Eva picks up the bread knife, looks at it, then at one of the kitchen drawers. She rises, unseen by Geoffrey, crosses to the drawer and, half opening it, wedges the knife inside so the point sticks out. She measures out a run and turns to face the knife. Geoffrey, still talking, is now watching her absently. Eva works up speed and then takes a desperate run at the point of the knife. Geoffrey, belatedly realizing what she's up to, rushes forward, intercepts her and reseats her.*)

GEOFFREY: Eva, now for heaven's sake! Come on . . . (*He studies her nervously.*) Look, I'm going to phone the doctor. I'll tell him you're very upset and overwrought. (*He backs away and nearly impales himself on the knife. He grabs it.*) He can probably give you something to calm you down a bit. (*The doorbell rings.*) Oh, God, somebody else. Now, I'm going to phone the doctor. I'll just be two minutes, all right? Now, you sit here. Don't move, just sit there like a good girl. (*Opening the door and calling off.*) Would you mind helping yourselves in? I just have to make one phone call . . .

(*Geoffrey goes out. Silence. Eva finishes another note. A brief one. She tears it out and weighs it down, this time with a tin of dog food which happens to be on the table. She gazes around, surveying the kitchen. She stares*) *at the oven. She goes to it and opens it, looking inside thoughtfully. She reaches inside and removes a casserole dish, opens the lid, wrinkles her nose and carries it to the draining board. Returning to the oven, she removes three shelves and various other odds and ends that seem to have accumulated in there. It is a very dirty oven. She looks at her hands, now grimy, goes to the kitchen drawer and fetches a nearly clean tea towel. Folding it carefully, she lays it on the floor of the oven. She lies down and sticks her head inside, as it trying it on for size. She is apparently dreadfully uncomfortable. She wriggles to find a satisfactory position. The door opens quietly and Jane enters. The hubbub outside has now died down to a gentle murmur so not much noise filters through. Jane carries rather carefully two more glasses she considers dirty. She closes the door. She looks round the kitchen but sees no one. She crosses, rather furtively, to the sink and rinses the glasses. Eva throws an oven tray on to the floor with a clatter. Jane, startled, takes a step back and gives a little squeak. Eva, equally startled, tries to sit up in the oven and hits her head with a clang on the remaining top shelf.)*

JANE: (*Covering.*) Mrs. Jackson, are you all right? You shouldn't be on the cold floor in your condition, you know. You should be in bed. Surely? Here . . . (*She helps Eva to her feet and steers her back to the table.*) Now, you sit down here. Don't you worry about that oven now. That oven can wait. You clean it later. No point in damaging your health for an oven, is there? Mind you, I know just what you feel like, though. You suddenly get that urge, don't you? You say, I must clean that oven if it kills me. I shan't sleep, I shan't eat till I've cleaned that oven. It haunts you. I know just that feeling. I'll tell you what I'll do. Never say I'm not a good neighbor — shall I have a go at it for you? How would that be? Would you mind? I mean, it's no trouble for me, I quite enjoy it, actually — and you'd do the same for me, wouldn't you? Right. That's settled. No point in wasting time, let's get down to it. Now then, what are we going to need? Bowl of water, got any oven cleaner have you? Never mind, we'll find it — I hope you're not getting cold, you look very peaky.

(Hunting under the sink.) Now then, oven cleaner? Have we got any? Well, if we haven't, we'll just use our old friend Mr. Vim, won't we? *(She rummages.)*

(The door opens: Geoffrey enters and goes to Eva. Conversation is heard in the background.)

GEOFFREY: Darling, listen, it looks as if I've got . . . *(Seeing Jane.)* Oh.

JANE: Hallo, there.

GEOFFREY: Oh, hallo — anything you — want?

JANE: I'm just being a good neighbor, that's all. Have you by any chance got an apron I could borrow?

GEOFFREY: *(Rather bewildered, pointing to the chair.)* Er — yes — there.

JANE: Oh, yes. *(Putting it on.)* Couldn't see it for looking.

GEOFFREY: Er — what are you doing?

JANE: Getting your oven ready for tomorrow, that's what I'm doing.

GEOFFREY: For what?

JANE: For your Christmas dinner. What else do you think for what?

GEOFFREY: Yes, well, are you sure . . . ?

JANE: Don't you worry about me. *(She bustles around singing loudly, collecting cleaning things and a bowl of water.)*

GEOFFREY: *(Over this, irritated.)* Oh, Darling — Eva, look I've phoned the doctor but he's not there. He's apparently out on a call somewhere and the fool of a woman I spoke to has got the address and no number. It'll be quicker for me to try and catch him there than sitting here waiting for him to come back. Now, I'll be about ten minutes, that's all. You'll be all right, will you?

JANE: Don't you fret. I'll keep an eye on her. *(She puts on a rubber glove.)*

GEOFFREY: Thank you.

(He studies the immobile Eva. On a sudden inspiration, crosses to the kitchen drawer and starts taking out the knives. He scours the kitchen, gathers up the sharp instruments. Jane watches him, puzzled.)

GEOFFREY: *(By way of explanation.)* People downstairs are having a big dinner party. Promised to lend them some stuff.

JANE: Won't they need forks?

GEOFFREY: No. No forks. They're Muslims. *(As he goes to the door.)* Ten minutes.

(The doorbell rings.)

JANE: There's somebody.

GEOFFREY: The Brewster-Wrights, probably.

JANE: Oh . . .

(Geoffrey goes out, the dog barking as he does so, until the door closes.)

****

from **The Norman Conquests: Table Manners** (1973)

CHARACTERS

Norman
Sarah
Annie
Reg

[From the beginning of Act One, Scene Two, Norman is persona non grata since it has been revealed that he planned to have a weekend fling with his wife's sister. The silent treatment everyone is trying to give Norman provides a marvelously realistic reason for what is usually quite artificial on stage: the monologue. One must envision the reactions of the other characters to Norman's verbal assault to grasp the comic effect this scene has in performance.]

> *(The dining room. Sunday morning, 9 am. Norman is standing in his pajamas and bare feet. He is whistling. After a moment, Sarah, fully dressed, comes in with a tray of breakfast things.)*

NORMAN: (*Cheerfully.*) Morning.
SARAH: (*Seeing him.*) Oh. (*She unloads the tray, ignoring him.*)
NORMAN: Lovely morning. Hear the birds?

> *(Sarah continues grimly with her task.)*

NORMAN: Sleep well? Hope you slept well. I slept well.

> *(Sarah goes out. Norman starts to whistle again and examines what she has put on the table. Annie enters. She carries another tray of breakfast things.)*

NORMAN: Morning.

ANNIE: (*Seeing him.*) Oh. (*Annie starts unloading the tray, ignoring him.*)

NORMAN: Lovely morning. Sleep well, did you? I slept like a log. Must have been that wine. Wonderful. It's a rotten drink but it makes a lovely sleeping draught. I'd market it. Sleep nature's way with our dandelion brew. Arhar . . .

(*Annie goes out passing Sarah coming in with the last of the breakfast things.*)

NORMAN: What have we got for breakfast, then? What have we got?

SARAH: (*Calling.*) Reg? Breakfast.

REG: (*Offstage, distant.*) Right . . .

NORMAN: How's old Reg this morning? All right, is he? Sleep well, did he? . . . I can tell you I can do with some breakfast. Missed my meal last night. Did you know that? I missed my meal. I didn't hear the dinner gong. What sort of hotel do you call this?

(*Annie returns.*)

SARAH: Have you taken Mother hers up?

ANNIE: Yes.

NORMAN: I'll sit here, shall I? All right if I sit here? Anybody any objections if I sit here? (*He is ignored.*) I'll sit here.

(*Norman sits at the head of the table. Sarah sits at the other end with Annie close to her, isolating Norman. Norman sits whistling. Reg enters.*)

REG: (*Cheerily.*) Morning all.

NORMAN: Morning.

REG: (*His face falling.*) Oh.

(*Reg sits next to Sarah. Annie and Reg have cereal. Sarah butters toast.*)

NORMAN: Well, you're a right cheery lot, aren't you? Look at you. A right cheery lot. Woo-hoo . . . halloo . . . (*He waves at them.*)

SARAH: (*Acid.*) Nobody in this house is speaking to you ever again.

NORMAN: Oh, I see. I see. That's the way the Swiss rolls. I see. That's the way the apple crumbles, is it? Oh ho. That's the way the corn flakes . . . (*A pause. He ponders. Suddenly sharply.*) Sarah! Be careful! The butter . . .

SARAH: (*Alarmed.*) What?

NORMAN: Ha-ha! You spoke to me. Caught you. Caught you. (*Pause.*) All right, I'll talk to myself then. (*Very rapidly, in two voices.*) Hallo Norman — good morning, Norman — how are you, Norman — I'm very well, Norman — that's good news, Norman —

ANNIE: Shut up, Norman.

NORMAN: Ha-ha! Caught you again. That's two of you. Just got to catch Reg now. Two out of three. Just Reg left . . . (*Slight pause.*) Look out, Reg! (*No reaction.*) Ah — can't catch him that way. (*Sharply.*) Hey, Reg! . . . oh well. If that's the way it is. Don't talk to me. I don't care. Doesn't bother me. I don't know why you're all being so unsocial. All right, I had a few drinks last night. What's wrong with that? Hasn't anyone round this table ever had a drink then? Come on, I don't believe it. You've had a drink haven't you Reg? Ha-ha! Ha-ha! Caught you. You spoke.

REG: No, I didn't.

NORMAN: Ha-ha! Three to me. I've won. (*Pause.*) Nothing wrong in a few drinks. Don't speak. I don't care. Going to be a pretty dull Sunday if we all sit in silence, I can tell you. Well, I'm not sitting in silence. I'll find something to do. I know, I'll go up and frighten Mother.

(*Sarah looks up sharply and gives him a terrible glare.*)

NORMAN: Ah-ha! Nearly got you again. Is it too much to ask for something to eat? (*No response.*) It's too much to ask for something to eat. (*He gets up and moves down the table and takes the cereal bowl that Sarah isn't using.*) May I borrow your bowl? That's awfully nice of you. And your spoon? Thank you. Now then, what shall I have? (*Examining cereal packets.*) Puffa Puffa rice. Ah-ha . . . (*He returns to the top of the table, sits and fills his bowl.*) No Sunday papers. Dear, dear. Ah, well I shall have to read my morning cereal . . . (*He laughs.*) Cereal. Do we all get that? Apparently we don't. (*He reads. Suddenly, violently banging the table.*) Stop!

(*The others jump involuntarily.*)

NORMAN: Stop everything. Listen. A free pair of pinking shears for only 79p and six Puffa Puffa tokens. Hurry, hurry, hurry. What's this? Is nobody hurrying? Do you mean to tell me that none of you want them? Where's the spirit of British pinking? Dead, presumably. Like my relations. (*He eats a handful of dry cereal thoughtfully.*) Hang on, I've got another game. Mind reading. I'll read your minds. Now then, where shall we start? Sarah. Sarah is thinking — that noisy man up there should be home with his wife. What is he doing shattering the calm of our peaceful Sunday breakfast with his offers of reduced price pinking shears? Why is he here, shouting at us like this? Why isn't he at home, like any other decent husband, shouting at his wife? He came down here to seduce his wife's own sister. How low can he get? The fact that his wife's own sister said, at one stage anyway, that she was perfectly happy to go along with him is beside the point. The fact that little Annie here was perfectly happy to ditch old reliable Tom — without a second thought — and come off with me is beside the point. We won't mention that because it doesn't quite fit in with the facts as we would like them. And what is little Annie thinking, I wonder? Maybe furtively admiring my pajamas, who knows? Pajamas that could have been hers. With all that they contain. These nearly were mine. Or maybe she is thinking . . . Phew, that was a close shave. I could have been shacked up in some dreadful hotel with this man — at this very moment . . . what a lucky escape for me. Thank heavens, I am back here at home amidst my talkative family exchanging witty breakfast banter. Knowing my two-legged faithful companion and friend, Tom the rambling vet, is even now planning to propose to me in 1997 just as soon as he's cured our cat. Meanwhile, I can live here peacefully, totally fulfilled, racing up and down stairs looking after Mother, having the time of my life and living happily ever after until I'm fifty-five and fat . . . I'm glad I didn't go to that hotel. Well, let me tell you so am I. I wouldn't want a weekend with you, anyway. And I'll tell you the funniest thing of all, shall I? . . .

(Annie gets up and runs out.)

NORMAN: *(Yelling furiously after her.)* I didn't even book the hotel. I knew you wouldn't come. You didn't have the guts.

(A pause.)

SARAH: You can be very cruel, can't you Norman?

(Sarah goes out after Annie.)

NORMAN: Oh well. It's a bit quieter without those two. Hear yourself speak. Too damned noisy before. All that crunching of toast. Like a brigade of Guards marching on gravel. Well now, Reg —

(Reg chews glumly through his cereal.)

NORMAN: *(Looking round the table.)* Milk? Ah. *(He gets up.)* Sugar? *(He returns with these and sits. Pouring milk over his cereal.)* Nice peaceful morning. Just the two of us and — hark! the soft crackle of my Puffa Puffa rice. 'Tis spring indeed. *(Slight pause.)* I suppose you think I'm cruel too, don't you? Well, I've damn good cause to be, haven't I? I mean, nobody's thought about my feelings, have they? It's all Annie — Annie — Annie . . . what about me? I was going to give her everything. Well, as much as I could. My whole being. I wanted to make her happy for a weekend, that's all. I wanted to give her . . . *(Angrily.)* It was only for a few hours for God's sake. Saturday night, back on Monday morning. That was all it was going to be. My God! The fuss. What about your wife, Norman? What about my wife? Don't you think I'd take Ruth away, just the same? If she'd come. But she won't. She has no need of me at all, that woman, except as an emotional punch bag . . . I tell you, if you gave Ruth a rose, she'd peel all the petals off to make sure there weren't any greenfly. And when she'd done that, she'd turn round and say, do you call that a rose? Look at it, it's all in bits. That's Ruth. If she came in now, she wouldn't notice me. She'd probably hang her coat on me . . . It's not fair, Reg. Look, I'll tell you. A man with my type of temperament should really be ideally square jawed, broad shouldered, have blue twinkling eyes, a chuckle in his voice and a spring in his stride. He should get through three women a day without even ruffling his hair. That's what I'm like inside. That's my appetite. That's me. I'm a three a day man. There's enough of me in here to give. Not just sex, I'm talking about everything. The trouble is, I was born in the wrong damn body. Look at me. A gigolo trapped in a haystack. The tragedy of my life Norman Drewers — gigolo and assistant librarian. What's inside you, Reg? Apart from twelve bowls of cornflakes? What do you feel with Sarah? Do you sometimes feel like saying to her, no this is me. The real me. Look at me . . .

(Reg finishes his cornflakes.)

REG: I'll tell you something, Norman. You're a nice bloke. You've got your faults but you're a nice bloke but I think you must be the last person in the world I ever want to have breakfast with again.
NORMAN: Oh.

[SCENE CONTINUES]
****

from **Intimate Exchanges** (1982)

CHARACTERS

Celia Teasdale
Lionel Hepplewick
Sylvie Bell

[At the end of the opening scene, "How It All Began," the head-master's wife either does or does not have a cigarette. The following is the opening from "A Gardener Calls" — what happens when she does decide to have a cigarette. Note that she just misses Miles Coombes. Remember, two actors play all the characters. Comparing these two scenes provides a clear example of Ayckbourn's technical control of action, character, and dialogue.]

CELIA: (*Weakening.*) Oh, what the hell. (*She snatches up the cigarettes and lighter, lights one and perches on the edge of the table. She inhales. It has obviously been some hours since her last cigarette and it is a pleasurable experience.*)

(*The doorbell rings from within the house.*)

CELIA: (*Irritably.*) Oh, no. (*Calling.*) Sylvie, could you see who that is? If you're not in the loft. (*She waits.*) Sylvie? (*The doorbell rings again.*) Oh. (*She grinds out the cigarette rather crossly, as she says.*) All right then, I'll go. I'll go.

(*Before she can do so, Lionel Hepplewick comes on to the patio from the house. In his early thirties, he has the healthy complexion of a man who spends much of his life in the open air. Whilst being both pleasant and sub-servient in his manner, he has at the same time a secretive air of someone who knows more about you than he should.*)

LIONEL: Good afternoon, Mrs. Teasdale.

CELIA: Oh, Mr. Hepplewick. Nice to see you.

LIONEL: (*To Sylvie, presumably somewhere behind him.*) Thank you very much. (*To Celia.*) I hope this is not inconvenient?

CELIA: No, No. Sylvie and I were just — er — spring-cleaning. Well, something of the sort.

LIONEL: Midsummer cleaning. (*He smiles.*)

CELIA: (*Laughing.*) Yes, yes. (*Slight pause.*) Heavenly day.

LIONEL: Oh, yes.

CELIA: I hope it stays like this.

LIONEL: Yes.

CELIA: After that winter.

LIONEL: Yes. It'll stay like this till Thursday.

CELIA: Will it?

LIONEL: You'll get a bit of a cloud then late afternoon, maybe a spot of rain. That'll have cleared up by Friday. A bit breezy Saturday, but Sunday'll be a real scorcher.

CELIA: Really, really.

LIONEL: That's just my guess, mind you.

CELIA: You ought to do the weather forecasts on television.

(*Lionel makes a scornful noise.*)

CELIA: Anyway, excuse the mess. Now what can I do for you, Mr. — Lionel, isn't it? Yes, of course it's Lionel.

LIONEL: I just come round like I promised, Mrs. Teasdale.

CELIA: Like you . . . ? I'm sorry, I . . .

LIONEL: Oh, you may not remember. A few weeks ago, at the end of last term you may recall, we were talking — yourself, Mr. Teasdale and me — and you mentioned then, if I should have any spare time, I should come up and have a look at your garden.

CELIA: Yes, of course. It was a little while ago.

LIONEL: Now I've got the cricket pitches marked and the outfields mown, I thought I'd just come up and have a look. If that's all right.

CELIA: (*Without enthusiasm.*) Yes, of course. Well. There it is.

LIONEL: Yes.

CELIA: Neither of us are particularly garden-minded, I'm afraid.

LIONEL: (*Impassively.*) No.

CELIA: We love sitting in them, getting all the benefits. We both loathe any kind of hard work, I'm afraid. Still, what do you think?

LIONEL: (*After staring a moment.*) That's a useful shed.

CELIA: Oh, yes. The shed. That's a mess too, I'm afraid. It was put up by our predecessors, the last Headmaster and his wife, Mr. and Mrs. Cowlishaw. Now he was a keen gardener, Mr. Cowlishaw. He'd have been before your time.

LIONEL: Oh, yes.

CELIA: Yes, your father would have been school caretaker then, wouldn't he?

LIONEL: He would, yes.

CELIA: He's still well, is he — er — Joe? Is Joe keeping fit?

LIONEL: Very well, thank you. He's still got his knee troubles but he's a fine old man.

CELIA: Oh, yes. Is he coping without your mother?

LIONEL: Just about.

CELIA: Still, it was a long illness.

LIONEL: It was a very long illness. It was a relief to see her die, I don't mind saying.

CELIA: Yes.

LIONEL: (*Holding out his hand and clenching his fist.*) She was like that when she died.

CELIA: Was she? Was she? (*Slight pause.*) Like what exactly?

LIONEL: Like the size of my hand, she was. Fifteen stone woman shrunk down to that.

CELIA: Oh, dear.

LIONEL: The size of that.

CELIA: Yes, yes. (*Pause.*) Well . . .

LIONEL: Yes, we can do something with this, I don't doubt.

CELIA: Would you like to take a look around?

LIONEL: Thank you very much.

CELIA: I mean, there isn't much. What you see is what we have. I'll make some coffee. Would you like some coffee? Or tea? There's tea.

LIONEL: Cup of tea would be very pleasant, thank you, Mrs. Teasdale.

CELIA: Right. Tea. I won't be a moment. (*She begins to move inside.*)

LIONEL: Be all right for me to go in the shed, will it?

CELIA: Yes, help yourself. It shouldn't be locked.

(*Celia goes into the house. Lionel prowls around the garden, tutting a little, as he examines it more closely. As he reaches the bottom of the garden, he sees someone beyond the hut in the playing field.*)

LIONEL: (*Calling.*) Afternoon, Mr. Coombes. Very well, thank you. . . . She's just gone in the house. Did you want to speak to her? . . . Right, just as you like. (*He watches whomever it was he was talking to walking away, with a slight look of contempt. He then starts to pace the garden out and appears to be doing calculations in his head.*)

(*Sylvie comes out of the house. She is a young, fresh-faced awkward girl but not unattractive. Like Celia, she is dressed for heavy housework.*)

[SCENE CONTINUES]
****

CHARACTERS

> Celia Teasdale
> Miles Coombes

[The following is the opening from "A Visit from a Friend" — what happens when she decides not to have to a cigarette. Note that she just misses Lionel Hepplewick.]

(*In this instance, Celia resists the temptation and virtuously goes off down the garden and into the shed. Although the inside of this is not much vis-*

ible during this particular scene, we hear her from the inside and gather it is fairly cluttered with junk.)

CELIA: (*In the shed.*) Oh, God. (*She clumps about looking for something.*)

(Sound of the front doorbell. Celia, not hearing it, carries on sorting.)

CELIA: (*In the shed.*) I mean, honestly . . . How is anyone expected to . . . (*She grunts as she heaves something heavy down.*) . . . find anything in this . . . uggh. (*She clumps and grunts some more.*)

(Sound of the front doorbell. The noises in the shed stop. Celia sticks her head out of the shed door and listens, uncertain if she heard anything or not. Hearing nothing more, she goes back into the shed. A moment later, she emerges with a stepladder. Closing the shed door, she lugs the ladder back toward the house. Again, she passes the cigarettes on the patio. Again, she pauses, tempted. She stands, deliberating. Miles Coombes enters. He is a lean, rather sad man about the same age as Celia.)

MILES: Celia.

CELIA: Oh, hallo, Miles.

MILES: How are things?

CELIA: Super. Was that you?

MILES: I'm sorry.

CELIA: Was that you ringing?

MILES: No.

CELIA: The doorbell.

MILES: No.

CELIA: Just now.

MILES: No.

CELIA: I thought I heard somebody.

MILES: I don't think it was me. No, it couldn't have been. Hang on, it could have possibly been Hepplewick.

CELIA: Hepplewick.

MILES: You know, Lionel Hepplewick. I thought I saw him stomping away a minute ago.

CELIA: Oh. Really. Wonder what he wanted.

MILES: You're looking busy.

CELIA: Yes. I'm taking down the sitting-room curtains.

MILES: Ah. Yes.

CELIA: Sylvie and I are just having a clear out.

MILES: Spring cleaning.

CELIA: In June, yes. Better late than never.

MILES: Er — Celia. Have you a minute to spare?

CELIA: Not really, no.

MILES: (*Stymied.*) Oh. All right then.

(*Pause.*)

CELIA: If you don't mind, Miles, we're frightfully busy.

MILES: Yes.

CELIA: I mean, I'm absolutely . . . we're absolutely . . . well, we're completely. . . . (*Irritably.*) You can see we are, surely?

MILES: Oh, yes, yes, yes. No, no, no. Doesn't matter. No, no.

(*A silence. Miles continues to stand there.*)

CELIA: It's obviously important.

MILES: Yes, well . . .

CELIA: Oh, Lord. OK. (*She stands, still holding the steps.*)

MILES: Do you want to put those down?

CELIA: (*Ignoring this suggestion.*) It's not something you could possibly talk to Toby about, is it?

MILES: Not really, no.

CELIA: Oh.

MILES: It's really about Toby, you see.

CELIA: Oh, why talk to me, Miles? Why me?

MILES: You're his wife, Celia, for one thing.

CELIA: Yes, I know but . . . there's nothing I can say. What Toby does is his own concern. Talk to him.

MILES: It's more than just Toby. It's the school as well, Celia, I'm talking about the school.

CELIA: Then talk to the Headmaster. I'm only his wife. I don't have any influence. I'm just an honorary non-voting, non-participating . . . thing in the background. There's no point in talking to me, Miles. Honestly there isn't.

MILES: That isn't true, Celia, you know it. (*After a pause.*) You're certainly not a thing. (*After a pause.*) Look. Look, I'm taking the gloves off now, Celia, and I'm going to put all the cards on the table and I'm going to be absolutely frank. Now, I'm wearing my Chairman of the Board of Governors hat at the moment, all right?

CELIA: Hat, no gloves.

MILES: Sorry?

CELIA: Look, I've left Sylvie in the loft.

MILES: You're the absolute hub of this place, you know that, Celia. The rack and pinion of this establishment. The whole institution would cave in without you.

CELIA: Rubbish.

MILES: Everyone comes to you with their troubles. . . .

CELIA: Well, they do that, yes. Because I'm stupid enough to listen.

MILES: The staff come to you. The kids come to you. The parents.

CELIA: The parents certainly do.

MILES: Well, then. You're marvelous. Not a non-participating thing at all. Very much the reverse. If Toby only had one quarter of that.

CELIA: I'm sorry. I'm not prepared to start talking about Toby.

MILES: Yes, that shows great loyalty. Great loyalty.

CELIA: Nothing to do with loyalty. I'm just sick to death talking about him. Let's talk about me.

MILES: Just one micro-second, I promise you.

CELIA: (*Reluctantly.*) Well, wait there a minute. I'll have to go and sort Sylvie out first. She's straddled up there in the rafters.

MILES: Do you want me to . . . ?

CELIA: No, for heaven's sake don't come in here, it's frightful. I'll be back. (*Then, as an afterthought.*) Oh, could you fish a couple of chairs out of the shed?

MILES: Yup.

(Celia goes into the house with the stepladder.)

MILES: (*After she's gone, rather lamely:*) Don't be too long, will you? I've got a meeting in a few . . . oh. (*His voice trails away and he mutters to himself.*) Got to talk to the Board. (*Miles wanders toward the shed, still muttering to himself. At first, these mutterings seem fairly incomprehensible but then it transpires he's running over his speech.*) Meeuurrr . . . meeuurrr . . . nah-nah-nah-nah . . . meeuurrr . . . nah, ladies and gentle of the Board . . . here is a . . . meeuurrr who over the meeuurrr has been nah-meeuurrr and meeuurrr. Hair-hore . . . therefore . . . (*He opens the door to the shed and pauses.*) . . . therefore, before we rush into this . . . no, before we leap into this . . . before we jump to — jump to hasty judgments — conclusions. Rush into any hasty conclusions, let us be quite certain, let's be perfectly certain . . . (*He finds two fold-up chairs just inside the shed and pulls them out.*) no, let us be sure that we're not attempting to lay the blame for something at the door of a man . . . at the feet of a man . . . at the head of a man . . . heap the blame on a man's feet . . . no, on his head. Can't heap blame on his feet . . . on a man who is himself limbless . . . no, blameless . . . oh, hell. (*He stands in the doorway of the shed, having reached an impasse with his speech.*)

(Celia comes out of the house.)

CELIA: I've put the kettle on. Like a cup of something, would you?
MILES: Oh, thanks. I think I've just got time. Here. (*He proffers the chairs.*)
CELIA: Oh, well.

[SCENE CONTINUES]
****

from **Private Fears in Public Places** (2004)

from assorted scenes

CHARACTERS

Nicola

Dan

[Made up of fifty-four scenes about the interconnected lives of seven characters and as many relationships, the following are three scenes featuring Nicola and Dan. Here Ayckbourn's use of humor is quite subtle as he continues to explore his oft-pursued subject of relationships.]

(The action takes place in various flats, an office, a sitting room, a kitchen, a café and a hotel bar. Now. A period of several days.)

SCENE FOUR

(Nicola's flat. Dan slumped in a chair, Nicola being busy.)

NICOLA: . . . No, as I say, I was hanging around for ages. With this man. This wretched house agent. I mean, I have far better things to do in my lunch hour. Having lunch, for one thing. I mean all I got in the end was a roll. I'm starving.

DAN: You can't survive on a roll.

NICOLA: I certainly can't. I don't know about anyone else. So. Where were you?

DAN: Oh, I was, you know, mooching about.

NICOLA: Drinking.

DAN: No. Not really. Well, a bit of drinking. Not a lot of drinking, you know.

NICOLA: I thought you were supposed to be looking for a job.

DAN: Come on, give us a chance.

NICOLA: Have you any more interviews?

DAN: (*Vaguely.*) I've got one on Thursday, I think. For a brewery.

NICOLA: That should suit you down to the ground.

****

CHARACTERS

Nicola

Dan

SCENE EIGHTEEN

(Nicola's flat. It is dark. Dan creeps in, still drunk.)

DAN: (*From the darkness — *) . . . Nicola . . . Nicola, old thing! You asleep darling? Nicola? Nicky? (*Pause.*) Oh, God. Alright. Be like that, I don't care. See if I care.

(An almighty crash as Dan falls over something.)

DAN: Oh, SHIT. Ow. (*Pause.*) Ow! Ow! Ow! Nicola! I think I may have broken my leg. Nicola. I've broken my leg. Don't you care, I've broken my leg? God, you can be a hard woman sometimes. You really can. I'm going to sleep in the hall, do you hear? It'll be a damn sight warmer than getting into bed with you, I can tell you. I'm going in the hall. With my broken leg.

(Dan goes out. Another crash.)

DAN: (*Offstage.*) Ow! (*In a little-boy voice.*) I've broken my arm now? Nicky?

NICOLA: (*From the darkness, groaning.*) Oh, no . . .

(The lights cross-fade.)

****

CHARACTERS

Nicola

Dan

Stewart

SCENE TWENTY

(Another flat. Nicola and Dan. They are staring around them.)

DAN: It's tiny.

NICOLA: No, it isn't.

DAN: It's minute.

NICOLA: I rather like it.

DAN: I'm not living in it. Besides. Two bedrooms. We wanted three. What's he doing, showing us two-bedroomed places?

NICOLA: I said we'd — consider — two-bedroomed.

DAN: Did you?

NICOLA: They're very thin on the ground. Apparently, three-bedroomed. So he says.

DAN: What the hell does he know?

NICOLA: He's an estate agent.

DAN: He's only saying that because he hasn't got any three-bedroomed on his books. He's talking bollocks. You tell him from me he's talking bollocks. You tell him that.

NICOLA: You tell him. Why should I tell him? Go on, he'll be back in a minute, you tell him.

DAN: The papers are stuffed — absolutely crammed — with three-bedroomed flats.

NICOLA: Nonsense.

DAN: Walk past any estate agent's window and there's piles of them. Absolutely plastered with three-bedroomed places.

NICOLA: How do you know?

DAN: I know. I've walked past them. I've seen for myself.

NICOLA: Then why didn't you go in?

DAN: What?

NICOLA: Why didn't you go in and inquire? Instead of leaving it all to me? Why don't you do something for a change? You say, you see these flats, you read about them in the paper — why don't you ring up or walk in?

DAN: Oh, come on, give us a chance.

NICOLA: No, I'm fed up, Dan, I really am. If you must know, I'm pissed to the nines.

(Silence.)

DAN: You're in a pretty foul mood, aren't you?

NICOLA: Well. *(Brief pause.)* So, you don't like this, then?

DAN: No, I don't. I've said. It's only got two bedrooms. I need a study. I don't ask for much. I leave the kitchen to you, I leave the living room to you, I leave the master bedroom to you, I leave the master bathroom to you —

NICOLA: Exactly, that's what I'm saying, you leave everything to me.

DAN: — but when it comes to the study I'm putting my bloody foot down, I'm sorry.

NICOLA: *(Muttering.)* I still don't know why you need one, I really don't.

DAN: What?

(Nicola doesn't reply.)

DAN: *(Sharply.)* What?

NICOLA: Don't say "What?" like that. You're just like our father when you do that. What? What? What? Every time you say anything to him. What? What? What?

DAN: What?

NICOLA: What?

DAN: What did you say? Just then?

NICOLA: It doesn't matter. *(Pause.)* Listen, why don't we have a guest bedroom that also doubles as a study?

DAN: Doubles?

NICOLA: So that when people come to stay, say, my sister, she could sleep in the study.

DAN: Where?

NICOLA: On the couch. Or whatever. You could get one of those pull-you-outs.

DAN: What?

NICOLA: Pull-you — things. They're sofas in the day time and then you sort of pull them and they flip, like that, and they become a bed.

DAN: I see. And my desk — what does that become? — a washstand, or something?

NICOLA: Don't be silly.

DAN: (*Angrily.*) I'm telling you. I want my own study with a door that closes. I want a desk with a swivel chair, I want a comfortable leather armchair with a matching footstool and a bookcase. I don't want pull-me-outs and sisters strewing their knickers all over my trophies. Now, you tell this bloke to get his finger out and line us up a few three-bedroomed flats pretty damn pronto or we're taking our business elsewhere.

NICOLA: You tell him.

DAN: I will.

(*Silence. Nicola looks out of the window. Dan sulks.*)

NICOLA: (*Rather sadly.*) It's a lovely view. Out of this window.

DAN: Is it? Jolly good.

(*Stewart enters, his mobile phone in his hand*)

STEWART: I'm so sorry, I do beg you pardon. (*Waving his mobile.*) Curse of the modern world, aren't they, these things? I mean, I don't know how we'd manage without them, but oh dear me, the trouble they cause. Now. What do we both think?

NICOLA: (*Looking at Dan.*) Well . . .

DAN: Well, we both rather feel — it's a bit small. For our requirements.

STEWART: I felt it might be. I did feel it might be. I did say to Nicola, didn't I, Nicola?

DAN: I think we were both hoping for a three-bedroom, you know, in order for —

STEWART: Happy future events.

DAN: What?

NICOLA: So he can go to sleep in the afternoons.

STEWART: Yes?

NICOLA: Like his father.

(Stewart laughs uncertainly. Dan moves away crossly.)

STEWART: Well, now, if we've seen all we need to see, perhaps we should move on.

NICOLA: Perhaps we should. I need to get back to work.

STEWART: After you, Nicola . . .

NICOLA: Thank you.

STEWART: After you — Dan.

(They go out. The lights cross-fade.)

****

Ayckbourn

THE READING ROOM

YOUNG ACTORS AND THEIR TEACHERS

Allen, Paul. *Alan Ayckbourn: Grinning at the Edge*. London: Methuen, 2001.

Billington, Michael. *Alan Ayckbourn*. 2nd ed. Macmillan Modern Dramatists. London: Macmillan, 1990.

Glaap, Albert Reiner. *A Guided Tour Through Ayckbourn Country*. 2nd ed. Trier, Germany: Wissenschaftlicher Verlag Trier, 2004.

Karensky, Oleg. *The New British Drama: Fourteen Playwrights Since Osborn and Pinter*. London: Hamish Hamilton, 1977.

Murgatroyd, Simon. *Alan Ayckbourn*. September 1, 2008, www.alanayckbourn.net.

Nightingale, Benedict. "Alan Ayckbourn." In *A Reader's Guide to Fifty Modern British Plays*, 431–438. London: Heinemann, 1982.

White, Sidney Howard. *Alan Ayckbourn*. Twayne English Authors Series. Edited by Kinley E. Roby. Boston: Twayne Publishers, 1984.

SCHOLARS, STUDENTS, PROFESSORS

Bartsch, Uta. *Alan Ayckbourns Dramenfiguren: Charakterisierung und Charakteristika*. Anglistische und amerikanistische Texte und Studien 1. Hildesheim, Germany: G. Olms Verlag, 1986

Becker, Peter von. "Der Fall Ayckbourn." In *Theater 1987*. Eds. Becker, Michael Merschmeier and Henning Rischbieter. Jahrbuch der Zeitschrift *Theater heute*. Zurich: Orell Fussli and Friedrich Verlag, 1987, 25–38.

Berger, Dieter A. "Asthetik des Spiels im zeitgenossischen britischen Drama." *Forum Modernes Theater* 3.1 (1988): 17–30.

This extensive bibliography lists books about the playwright according to whom the books might be of interest. If you would like to research further something that interests you in the text, lists of references, sources cited, and editions used in this book are found in this section.

Blistein, Elmer M. "Alan Ayckbourn: Few Jokes, Much Comedy." *Modern Drama* 26 (March 1983): 26–35.

Dukore, Bernard F. "Craft, Character, Comedy: Ayckbourn's *Women in Mind.*" *Twentieth Century Literature* 32 (Spring 1986): 23–39.

_____. "Alan Ayckbourn's Liza Doolittle." *Modern Drama* 32 (September 1989): 425–439.

Elsom, John. *Post-War British Theatre.* London: Routledge and Kegan Paul, 1976.

Holt, Michael. *Alan Ayckbourn.* Writers and Their Work Literary Conversation Series. Jackson: University Press of Mississippi, 1997.

Kalson, Albert E. *Laughter in the Dark: The Plays of Alan Ayckbourn.* Madison: Farleigh Dickinson University Press, 1993.

Page, Malcolm "The Serious Side of Alan Ayckbourn." *Modern Drama* 26 (March 1983): 36–46.

Taylor, John Russell. "Three Farceurs: Alan Ayckbourn, David Cregan, Simon Gray." In *The Second Wave,* 153–171. London: Methuen, 1971.

Watson, Ian, comp. *Alan Ayckbourn: Bibliography, Biography, Playography.* Theatre Checklist 21. London: TQ Publications, 1980.

THEATERS, PRODUCERS

Dukore, Bernard F. *Alan Ayckbourn: A Casebook.* New York: Garland Publishing, 1991.

Gussow, Mel. "Bard of the British Bourgeoisie." *New York Times Magazine,* January 28,1990, 23–24, 26–27, 84.

Hayman, Ronald. *British Theatre Scene Since 1955.* London: Oxford University Press, 1979.

Jarvis, Martin. *Broadway, Jeeves?* London: Methuen, 2003.

Taylor, John Russell. "Art and Commerce: The New Drama in the West End Marketplace." In *Contemporary English Drama.* Stratford-Upon-Avon Series 19. Edited by C. W. E. Bigsby, 177–187. London: Edward Arnold, 1981.

Wu, Duncan. *Six Contemporary Playwrights: Bennett, Gray, Brenton, Hare, Ayckbourn.* New York: Macmillan, 1996.

ACTORS, DIRECTORS, THEATER PROFESSIONALS

Allen, Paul. *A Pocket Guide to Alan Ayckbourn's Plays*. London: Faber and Faber, 2004

Joseph, Stephen. *New Theatre Forms*. London: Sir Isaac Pitman & Sons, 1968.

Joseph, Stephen. *Theatre in the Round*. London: Barrie and Rockliff, 1967.

Kalson, Albert E. "On Stage, Off Stage, and Backstage with Alan Ayckbourn." In *Themes in Drama* 10: *Farce*. Edited by J. Redmond, 251–258. Cambridge: Cambridge University Press, 1988.

Page, Malcolm. "Ayckbourn, Alan," In *Contemporary Dramatists*. Edited by D. L. Kirkpatrick. London: St. James Press, 1981.

Page, Malcolm, ed. *File on Ayckbourn*. Writer-Files. London, Methuen, 1989.

Smith, Leslie. "Farce and Contemporary Drama: I." In *Modern British Farce: A Selective Study of British Farce from Pinero to the Present*. London: Macmillan, 1989, 139–174.

Watson, Ian. *Conversations with Ayckbourn*. 2nd ed. London: Faber and Faber, 1988.

EDITIONS OF AYCKBOURN'S WORKS USED IN THIS BOOK

Ayckbourn, Alan. *Alan Ayckbourn, Plays 3: Haunting Julia, Sugar Daddies, Drowning on Dry Land, Private Fears in Public Places*. London: Faber & Faber, 2005.

_____. *Intimate Exchanges*. 2 vols. London: Samuel French, 1985.

_____. *The Norman Conquests*. New York: Doubleday, 1975.

_____. *Three Plays: Absurd Person Singular, Absent Friends, Bedroom Farce*. New York: Grove, 1994.

SOURCES CITED IN THIS BOOK

Allen, Paul. *Alan Ayckbourn: Grinning at the Edge*. London: Methuen, 2001.

Ayckbourn, Alan. *Alan Ayckbourn, Plays 3: Haunting Julia, Sugar Daddies, Drowning on Dry Land, Private Fears in Public Places*. London: Faber & Faber, 2005.

_____. *Damsels in Distress*. London: Faber & Faber, 2002.

_____. *House & Garden: Two Plays*. London: Faber & Faber, 2001.

_____. *How the Other Half Loves*. London: Samuel French, 1982.

_____. *Intimate Exchanges*. 2 vols. London: Samuel French, 1985.

_____. *Joking and Other Plays*. London: Chatto & Windus, 1979.

_____. *Revenger's Comedies*. London: Faber & Faber, 1991.

_____. *Ten Times Table*. London: Samuel French, 1981.

_____. *The Crafty Art of Playmaking*. London: Faber and Faber, 2002.

_____. *The Norman Conquests*. New York: Doubleday, 1975.

_____. *Three Plays: Absurd Person Singular, Absent Friends, Bedroom Farce*. New York: Grove, 1994.

_____. *Woman in Mind*. London: Faber & Faber, 1986.

Billington, Michael. "Life and Beth." *The Guardian*, July 23, 2008.

Connell, Brian. "A *Times* Profile Interview." *The Times* (London), May 5, 1976.

_____. "Playing for Laughs to a Lady Typist." *The Times* (London), January 5, 1976.

Coveney, Michael. "Scarborough Fare: An Interview with Alan Ayckbourn." *Play and Players*, September 1975.

Dukore, Bernard F. *Alan Ayckbourn: A Casebook*. New York: Garland Publishing, 1991.

_____. *Dramatic Theory and Criticism*. New York: Holt, 1974.

Gore-Langton, Robert. "Alan Ayckbourn: 'It's a Love-Hate Thing with Theatre." *The Times* (London), July 21, 2008.

Gussow, Mel. "Bard of the British Bourgeoisie." *New York Times*, January 28, 1990.

Isherwood, Charles. "All Are Together, and Everyone Is Alone." *New York Times*, June 15, 2005.

Kalson, Albert E. *Laughter in the Dark: The Plays of Alan Ayckbourn*. Madison: Farleigh Dickinson University Press, 1993.

McAfee, Annalena. *Evening Standard*, March 8, 1991.

Nightingale, Benedict. "Ayckbourn — Comic Laureate of Britain's Middle Class. *New York Times*, March 25, 1979.

Powell, Lucy. "Exit, the King: Is Alan Ayckbourn Set for One Glorious Final Act?" *The Independent*, August 24, 2008.

Priestly, J. B. *An Inspector Calls*. New York: Dramatists Play Service, 1998.

Spenser, Charles. *Daily Telegraph*, June 22, 1999.

Tinker, Jack. *Daily Mail*, August 2, 1974.

Watson, Ian. *Conversations with Ayckbourn*. 2nd ed. London: Faber and Faber, 1988.

White, Sidney Howard. *Alan Ayckbourn*. Twayne English Authors Series. Ed. Kinley E. Roby. Boston: Twayne Publishers, 1984.

The Ayckbourn awards list was found at
http://biography.alanayckbourn.net/BiographyAwards.htm.

Ayckbourn

MAJOR AWARDS

1973: Evening Standard Best Comedy Award *(Absurd Person Singular)*

1974: Evening Standard Best Play Award *(The Norman Conquests)*

1974: Play and Players Best Play Award *(The Norman Conquests)*

1974: Variety Club of Great Britain Playwright of the Year

1977: Evening Standard Best Play Award *(Just Between Ourselves)*

1979: Shared Plays and Players Best Comedy Award *(Joking Apart)*

1985: Evening Standard Best Comedy Award *(A Chorus of Disapproval)*

1985: Olivier Best Comedy Award *(A Chorus of Disapproval)*

1985: DRAMA Best Comedy Award *(A Chorus of Disapproval)*

1987: Evening Standard Best Play Award *(A Small Family Business)*

1988: Plays and Players Best Director Award *(A View from the Bridge)*

1989: Evening Standard Best Comedy Award *(Henceforward...)*

1990: Evening Standard Best Comedy Award *(Man of the Moment)*

1991: Drama-Logue Critic Award (LA) *(Henceforward...)*

1993: TMA/Martini Regional Theatre Award Best Show for Children & Young People *(Mr. A's Amazing Maze Plays)*

1993: Writers' Guild of Great Britain Lifetime Achievement Award

1993: Birmingham Press Club Personality of the Year Award

1993: John Ederyn Hughes Rural Wales Award for Literature

1994: Yorkshire Man of the Year

1994: Montblanc de la Culture Award for Europe

1996: TMA Regional Theatre Awards Best Musical *(By Jeeves)*

1996: Writers' Guild of Great Britain Best West End Play *(Communicating Doors)*

1997: Best Comedy *(Communicating Doors)*

1997: Lloyds Private Banking Playwright of the Year *(Things We Do for Love)*

2001: Sunday Times Award for Literary Excellence

2003: Moliere for Best Comedy *(Things We Do for Love)*

2004: Variety Club of Great Britain Lifetime Achievement Award

2005: Yorkshire Arts And Entertainment Personality Award (Yorkshire Awards 2005)

2009: Hall Of Fame for Achievements in American Theatre

2009: The Laurence Olivier Awards Special Award

2009: Outer Critics Circle Award for Outstanding Revival (The Norman Conquests)

2009: The New York Drama Critics' Circle Special Citation (The Norman Conquests)

2009: Drama Desk Award for Best Revival (The Norman Conquests)

2009: Tony for Best Revival of a Play (The Norman Conquests)

OTHER AWARDS AND HONORS

1987: CBE (Companion of the Order of the British Empire)

1997: KBE (Knight Companion of the Order of the British Empire)

1986: Freeman of the Borough of Scarborough

HONORARY DOCTORATES AND FELLOWSHIPS

1981: University of Hull (Hon. D. Litt.)

1982: Bretton Hall (Hon. Fellow)

1987: University of Keele (Hon. D. Litt.)

1987: University of Leeds (Hon. D. Litt)

1992: University of York (Doctor of the University)

1994: University of Bradford (Hon. D. Litt.)

1995: University of Cardiff (Hon. Fellow)

1998: Open University (Doctor of the University)

2003: University of Manchester (Hon. D. Litt)

Honorary Professor of the University of Hull

MAJOR NOMINATIONS

Oliviers (London)

1984: Best Comedy (Intimate Exchanges)

1987: Best Director (A View from the Bridge)

1988: Best Comedy (Henceforward . . .)

1990: Play of the Year (Man of the Moment)

1994: Best Comedy (Time of My Life)

1996: Best Comedy (Communicating Doors).

1996: Outstanding Musical Production (By Jeeves)

1998: Best Comedy *(Things We Do for Love)*
2000: Best Comedy *(Comic Potential)*
2003: Best Comedy *(RolePlay)*

Tonys (New York)
1978–79: Outstanding Direction of a Play (with Peter Hall) *(Bedroom Farce)*
1978–79: Best Play *(Bedroom Farce)*

Outer Critics Circle (New York)
2000: Outer Critics Circle Award for Outstanding Off-Broadway Play *(Comic Potential)*

Drama Desk (New York)
2000: Outstanding Play *(Comic Potential)*
2006: Outstanding Director of a Play *(Private Fears in Public Places)*

Drama League (New York)
2009: Distinguished Revival *(The Norman Conquests)*

INDEX

The entries in the index include highlights from the main In an Hour essay portion of the book.

ABOUT THE AUTHOR

E. Teresa Choate is an Associate Professor and Assistant Chair at the Department of Theatre in the College of Visual and Performing Arts at Kean University in Union, New Jersey. She teaches theater history and dramatic literature, performance theory, dramaturgy, and script analysis, as well as period styles of acting. She is also a director who has mounted over seventy productions to date. She holds an alphabet soup's worth of degrees in theater: PhD (UCLA), MFA in directing (Catholic University of America), MA (Denver University). She is currently the President of Alpha Psi Omega, the National Honor Theatre Society for colleges and universities.

NOTE FROM AUTHOR

Thanks go to Cliff Jewell, my husband, for his unconditional support, and to Kean University's Department of Theatre faculty, staff, and students for their support and encouragement.

Smith and Kraus would like to thank Casarotto Ramsay Associates, Ltd. and Faber and Faber / Faber, Straus & Giroux, whose enlightened permissions policy reflects an understanding that copyright law is intended to both protect the rights of creators of intellectual property as well as to encourage its use for the public good.

Know the playwright, love the play.

Open a new door to theater study, performance, and audience satisfaction with these Playwrights In an Hour titles.

ANCIENT GREEK

Aeschylus   Aristophanes   Euripides   Sophocles

RENAISSANCE

William Shakespeare

MODERN

Anton Chekhov   Noël Coward   Lorraine Hansberry
Henrik Ibsen   Arthur Miller   Molière   Eugene O'Neill
Arthur Schnitzler   George Bernard Shaw   August Strindberg
Frank Wedekind   Oscar Wilde   Thornton Wilder
Tennessee Williams

CONTEMPORARY

Edward Albee   Alan Ayckbourn   Samuel Beckett
Theresa Rebeck   Sarah Ruhl   Sam Shepard   Tom Stoppard
August Wilson

To purchase or for more information
visit our web site inanhourbooks.com